THE COVENANT PEOPLE

Turn to page 13.

THE
COVENANT PEOPLE

BY
MORDECAI I. SOLOFF

The first 2000 years
of Jewish life
From Abraham to Akiba

drawings by
CHAYA BURSTEIN

JONATHAN DAVID PUBLISHERS
MIDDLE VILLAGE, N. Y. 11379

THE COVENANT PEOPLE
by
Mordecai I. Soloff
Copyright© 1973
by
JONATHAN DAVID PUBLISHERS
Middle Village, N.Y. 11379

SECOND PRINTING
February 1975

Library of Congress Catalogue Card No. 72-97080
ISBN 0-8246-0154-8

Printed in the United States of America

The Brit

TO LIVE WITH HOPE

An unknown child wrote this poem. It was found in a Nazi concentration camp.

FROM
TOMORROW
ON

From tomorrow on
I shall be sad;

From tomorrow on.
Not today.
Today, I will be glad.
And every day,
No matter how bad
I shall say:
From tomorrow on
I shall be sad,
Not today.

Translated from the Yiddish

This child was a true member of THE COVENANT PEOPLE. He (or she) believed in the brit that Abraham made with God. He was full of hope and faith. He knew that even though today may be bad, tomorrow would be better.

This is what it means to a member of the covenant people. This is what the brit — the covenant or agreement — that Abraham made with God means to all Jews. It means that we live with faith and hope that the good things in life will prevail. Even if things are not going well today, they will be better tomorrow.

Table of Contents

UNIT THREE

UNIT FOUR

DO YOU KNOW WHO YOU ARE?

To the Student:

Jewish history is about 4,000 years old. That takes us back a long, long time!

Why should we want to learn about Jews who lived so long ago? What difference does it make who our ancestors were or how they lived?

How much can we possibly have in common with them?

The answer is simple. If we want to know who *we* are, we have to know *where* we came from. We have to know all about our ancestors.

We cannot have too many *things* in common with our ancestors, but we do have many *ideas* that we share. Abraham and Moses never saw television or rode in a car, but they did talk about God, and they did think about love and freedom.

We are concerned with these ideas too, and this is what we have in common with our ancestors. We have a religion in common; and that religion is called Judaism.

Judaism is one of the oldest and most respected religions in the world. It is a religion that started with Abraham, the first Jew. It is a religion that teaches us to be peaceful, to be fair, to be honest, and to be helpful to *all* human beings.

Everyone wants to know himself. In order for us to learn more about ourselves as Jews, we must find the key to unlock ourselves. We can do this by finding out why our ancestors thought it was necessary to teach all Jews to believe in God, to seek peace, and to be fair and honest.

Let's begin our search!

1

SPOTLIGHT ON UNIT ONE

3700 YEARS AGO ABRAHAM MADE A BRIT WITH GOD

ABRAHAM LED HIS TRIBE INTO THE PROMISED LAND — ERETZ YISRAEL

Introduction

ABRAHAM MAKES AN AGREEMENT

UNIT ONE will tell us about the people who were the first to become Jews. We will talk about some of the problems of our early ancestors from Abraham to Moses.

These early ancestors of ours were real people who faced real problems. The story of their lives is described in the first part of the Bible.

In this book we shall be calling the Bible by its Hebrew name: *Tanach*. The first part of the Bible, or Tanach, is called the *Torah*. The word Torah is also a Hebrew word.

The Torah, which consists of the first five books of the Tanach (Bible), is where we find almost all the information we have about our earliest ancestors.

Aside from all the interesting stories in the Torah about Abraham and Sarah and Isaac and Rebecca and Jacob and Leah and Rachel and Joseph and Moses and Aaron and Miriam and Joshua and all the rest of the

2

3500 YEARS AGO SOME JEWS LEFT TO SETTLE IN EGYPT.

THE EGYPTIANS LATER MADE SLAVES OF THEM.

3200 YEARS AGO MOSES LED THE JEWS OUT OF EGYPT.

THEY RENEWED THE COVENANT WITH GOD AND RECEIVED THE COMMANDMENTS AT SINAI.

familiar biblical characters, there is one part that is extremely important. It comes very early in the pages of the Tanach. It is the story of how God made an agreement with Abraham. We call that agreement the *covenant*. In Hebrew it is called the *brit*.

To our ancestors, from the days of Abraham and afterwards, the covenant, or agreement, was extremely important. And it is still important for us today. We shall discuss the covenant in this unit.

As you study this book, you may read some stories that you heard before. The story, as we tell it *here*, may not be told exactly as you heard it before. Do not be disturbed. The reason for this is that scientists are always discovering new information, and this is why the story may be different.

THE JEWISH TRIBES RETURNED TO ERETZ YISRAEL AND TOOK THE LAND.

TODAY YOU AND I CONTINUE TO KEEP THE JEWISH PEOPLE'S COVENANT WITH GOD.

3

Tourists travelling through the Negev Desert—
the land travelled by Abraham 4,000 years ago.

CHAPTER 1

WHEN ABRAHAM WAS YOUNG

Who Was Abraham?

Our Tanach tells us that the first man to become a Jew was Abraham.

Who was this man Abraham? How and why did he become a Jew? How did he get others to accept his ideas? When did all this happen?

Abraham was born on the continent of Asia, in a country once known as Mesopotamia, and later called Babylonia. Today, that part of the world is called Iraq.

In Abraham's times, many people lived in small villages. Their houses were tiny, and one house was quite far from another.

Many people who lived in those days had no fixed homes at all. They wandered about from place to place, and were called *nomads*. When nomads found a place they liked, they erected tents in which to eat and sleep. When they tired of a spot, they picked up and moved on.

Those who lived outside the villages got their food by hunting and fishing, by picking fruits and nuts, and by keeping flocks and herds. They also did some farming with very crude instruments.

5

The people of those early times not only had to find or grow their own food, they had to make their own clothes and build their own houses! When a person was fortunate enough to have extra food or extra tools, he might trade them for something someone else had.

In cities like Ur, where Abraham lived, the wealthier people lived in nice houses built for them by skilled builders. Land and labor and materials were paid for with gold, silver or copper rings. Various kinds of rings were accepted for payment just as we accept coins.

In the time of Abraham, in cities like Ur, records of business deals were kept. Some men were educated, and knew how to read and write. Since they had no paper in those days, they made marks on clay tablets or chiseled words on stone.

In recent years, many of those early records were found. They included business documents as well as stories and poems. They teach us a great deal about the times in which Abraham lived.

Abraham probably grew up in a very comfortable home. One story that has come down to us tells that Abraham's father made and sold statues. The people of those days called them *gods*, and we call them *idols*. Abraham discovered that these statues were not gods, and that they could not help anyone.

One day, Abraham saw some poor people in his father's shop buy some useless idols with their precious money-rings. This made Abraham very angry and he smashed all but one of his father's idols. In the hands of this idol he placed an axe, and then waited for his father to return.

"What happened?" shouted Terach, Abraham's father, when he saw his wrecked shop.

"He did it!" said Abraham, pointing to the idol with the axe.

"Stop that nonsense!" replied Terach. "This god can't move!"

"If so," said Abraham, "why do you call him god? Why do you worship him?"

We call this story a "legend" because we are not sure if it ever happened. But the very fact that this story was repeated over and over tells us that everyone considered Abraham to be a very bright and sensitive person. We know from the stories in the Torah that, unlike his father, Abraham did not become an idol-maker. Instead, he raised cattle and sheep.

Abraham Rejects Idol Worship

From the legend about Abraham breaking the idols, we may be sure that Abraham was not satisfied with the religion of the people of Ur. True, their place of worship was very impressive. It was a large, beautiful building. It seemed to tower high into the sky. The idols in their temple were often decorated with precious gold. Priests wore gorgeous robes, and musicians played many instruments. Sacrifices were offered with pomp and ceremony. But Abraham was not impressed.

Abraham Searches for God

The only religion Abraham ever knew was the one his parents believed in. He could not accept it. It disturbed him too much. He knew it was wrong to believe in many gods. Which of the many gods should a person believe in? The worshipers of many gods would always be confused. They would never know right from wrong. When something was pleasing to one god, it might be displeasing to another.

Abraham came to this conclusion: The only way for a man to know right from wrong, and to do what is good, is to worship *one* God.

Abraham did not believe it was wrong to offer animal sacrifices to God as a way of thanking him for the blessings of good health or good fortune. But Abraham was horrified at the common practice of sacrificing *children* to the gods.

Abraham's feelings were expressed in a well-known Bible story. One day he heard a command from God telling him to sacrifice his son, Isaac. Then, as he was about to obey the command, he was told *not* to touch his son. At the very last moment he was told that God did *not* want such sacrifices.

Abraham Takes a Trip to Paddan-Aram

Despite the comforts that Abraham enjoyed while living with his family in Ur, he became restless. One day, Abraham's father announced that the entire family would move to a new place—to Paddan-Aram, hundreds of miles to the north. On a modern map, Paddan-Aram lies in northern Syria.

Preparing to move a long distance was not easy in those days. Naturally, there were no moving-vans! People had to pack what they could on the backs of slow-moving donkeys. What they could not carry, they had to sell or leave behind. Sheep and cattle had to be driven on foot, and people had to walk. Only the weak, the aged, or the very young might ride on donkeys.

Also, they had no maps. The winding Euphrates River was the only guide for Abraham's family. There were some well-traveled roads, but they were not clearly marked or smooth. In addition, they could only follow routes where they might find food, and water and grass.

There were a few inns along the road, but travelers usually spent most nights outdoors. For shelter from the cold and rain, they would put up crude tents. When they were ready to move on, they would take them down.

To make a fire for cooking or for warmth, they chopped wood with bronze or stone axes. A fire was started by using glowing coals which they always carried with them. If by chance the coals died out, they would travel many extra miles to get a fresh supply, or would spend hours striking stones together to start a new one.

Food was carried in bags or in their garments, and water was stored in bottles made of skins. For cooking, they had to use pots of copper, bronze or clay.

The people who traveled with Abraham and his family faced many difficulties. The roads were not safe and they had to protect themselves. For this purpose, and also for hunting, they carried bows and arrows, axes, swords and knives — all made of bronze, copper or stone.

Abraham's family may have taken a full year to prepare for their journey, and another year to complete it. Yet it was done. Abraham and his family arrived safely in Paddan-Aram, and there they settled down among relatives and friends.

In our next chapter, we shall learn more about Abraham's adventures.

CHAPTER 2

ABRAHAM'S COVENANT WITH GOD

Eretz Yisrael—The Land of Israel

On the western coast of Asia, bordering on the Mediterranean Sea, lies a tiny country called Israel. In the eyes of the world it may appear small and unimportant. To us Jews, however, Israel is precious. Israel is the only country owned and governed by Jews. Although Moslems and Christians are citizens of Israel, most Israeli citizens are Jews. Almost all businesses, factories, and schools are owned and operated by Jews. Israel is a Jewish country to which (with few exceptions) any Jew, living anywhere in the world, is always welcome.

How and when did Israel become a Jewish country?

The Patriarch Abraham

The story begins with Abraham almost 4,000 years ago!

As you remember, Abraham moved from Ur in Babylonia to Paddan-Aram. Paddan-Aram was a pleasant place, and Abraham enjoyed life among his relatives and friends. His flocks and herds grew in number. He became the head of a group of people who were like a

Modern Bedouins travel with camels and donkeys, just as the nomads during Abraham's time did.

family, and were called a *tribe*. The head of the family was called the *patriarch* — which means, father-ruler. Members of the tribe were relatives, friends, servants, and others who wanted the patriarch's protection and help.

As patriarch, Abraham discussed problems with his tribesmen. He then made the final decision and announced the rules that were to govern the tribe. As patriarch, Abraham was also the religious leader of the tribe.

One of the problems that disturbed Abraham was the practice of idol-worship. He could not understand why people would want to worship many gods.

But what other kind of religion was there? He knew of none until . . . one day he was overcome by a strange feeling.

Turn to page 25

Abraham makes an Agreement

The Tanach (Bible) says that Abraham heard a voice. As soon as he heard it, he felt sure that it was the voice of the *one* God about whom he had been thinking. The voice was very clear to him. He distinctly heard it say:

> Go to another land that I, God, will show you—a land which will become yours and your children's forever. I will protect and guide you. I will make you into a great nation.

Abraham now knew what to believe. He was now certain that there was only *one* God. He was certain that people could trust this God, and that they could worship Him wholeheartedly. Abraham vowed that he and his descendants would follow this God faithfully.

After this experience, Abraham felt that he had now entered into an agreement with God. We call this agreement a *covenant*. In Hebrew it is called a *brit*. Abraham sealed the covenant by offering a sacrifice to God, and thus he became the first Jew. (In those early days a Jew was actually called a *Hebrew*.)

Abraham Spreads the News About the Brit

The patriarch Abraham then told his tribesmen of his brit with God. When they agreed to accept the brit, they too became Jews! And Abraham became the patriarch of the first Jewish tribe!

Later, Abraham adopted a permanent sign of the covenant. It was performed at a ceremony called *brit milah*. Every Jewish boy was to be circumcised on the eighth day after his birth. This was Abraham's way of reminding all Jews of their covenant with God.

To this very day, the son of a Jewish mother becomes a full Jew on the eighth day of his life when the ceremony of the brit milah is performed on him.

Abraham Moves to the Land of Israel

Faithful to his brit with God, Abraham decided to go to the land to which God had directed him. He informed his tribesmen of his plans, and they agreed to go with him.

Careful preparations were made, and the long, slow journey, filled with hardships and dangers, began. From Paddan-Aram, Abraham and his wife Sarah and the rest of his tribe crossed the great Euphrates River, and moved southward. After many months of difficult travel, they crossed the Jordan River into Eretz Yisrael—the Land of Israel. At that time, the land was called Canaan.

When Abraham came into Eretz Yisrael, he recognized it as *the* land to which God had directed him. In this land, Abraham and his tribesmen decided to make their home. This was to become his country and the country of his descendants.

Jews Become Nomads

The decision to settle in Eretz Yisrael was easier for the Jewish tribe to make than to carry out. The land was occupied by many unfriendly peoples: Canaanites, Amorites, Hittites, Jebusites, and others.

Some of these people lived in cities located in the northern and western parts of the country. Those cities were usually protected by thick walls. The gates of the cities were carefully guarded by day, and were firmly locked by night. Those who did not live in the cities, settled in villages. Others wandered about as nomads in the open spaces of the land.

Abraham and his newly arrived tribesmen were not welcomed by the old settlers. They called the Jews who had just come *Ivrim* (Hebrews). One of the possible meanings of this name is, "people who came from the other side" (meaning the *wrong* side) of the Euphrates river.

Abraham, however, was not troubled. He did not want to live too close to the Canaanites or close to any of the other strange, new people because they were all idol-worshippers. Each city, village, and nomadic tribe had a set of "gods," and everyone was expected to worship them. This, Abraham could not accept.

Abraham and his fellow tribesmen remembered their brit with God, and they decided to live by themselves. They moved out into the open country and settled down wherever there was sufficient food and water for their animals. When the grass withered or the wells dried up, the Hebrews (as they were now often called) picked up and moved on. At times, they moved because they learned of a better place, elsewhere. At other times, they would move because they wanted to avoid a fight.

To Live in Peace

Although Abraham was a peace-loving man, he was not afraid of a fight. The Tanach tells that a powerful league of kings once fought and defeated another league of kings who ruled over local cities. The victors carried away many captives. One of the captives was Lot, the nephew of Abraham. Abraham and his men attacked the armies of the victorious kings, defeated them, rescued Lot, and freed all the other captives.

To live peacefully was an important part of Abraham's belief in one God. Abraham's love of peace is clearly indicated in another Bible story. His nephew, Lot, owned many flocks of sheep and herds of cattle. He needed so much pasture-land for them that there was not much room left for Abraham's animals to graze.

An argument arose between the herdsmen who tended Abraham's cattle and the herdsmen who tended Lot's cattle. Each claimed the land, and wanted the other to leave.

Abraham, as patriarch, could have ordered Lot to remove his cattle. Instead he said:

> Let there be no strife, I pray, between me and you, and between my herdsmen and your herdsmen, for we are brothers.

Then Abraham suggested to Lot that he take his pick

of the land. Lot picked the land to the east, near the Jordan river, and Abraham stayed in the land of Canaan. The argument was settled, and Abraham continued to live in peace with his nephew.

Abraham Goes South

For a while, Abraham's tribe made its home in the Negev—in the southern part of Eretz Yisrael. But it was difficult for them, because the earth was parched. Water was scarce, and grassy areas were hard to find. The need to move was constant.

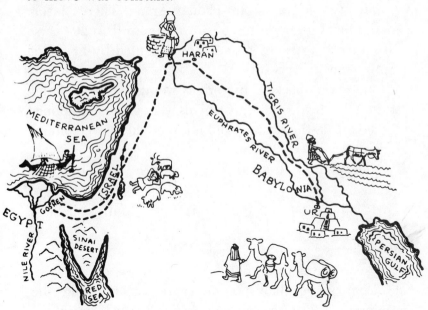

Abraham and his tribe were determined to live in Eretz Yisrael despite the hardships. However, after a long dry spell, they picked up and moved to Egypt. Happily for them, their stay in Egypt was rather brief. They learned from travelers that Eretz Yisrael was being blessed with much rain and they decided to return.

As time passed, Abraham's tribe grew larger and larger. At times, people from other tribes joined them as well.

After Abraham died, his son, Isaac, became the patriarch. Isaac had two sons: Jacob and Esau. Jacob became the patriarch after Isaac died.

Jacob Becomes Israel

The Tanach tells us that Jacob (son of Isaac), the grandson of Abraham, quarreled with his brother Esau. To avoid being killed, Jacob went off to grandfather Abraham's old home in Paddan-Aram. There, Jacob married and grew prosperous. After more than 20 years, he returned to Eretz Yisrael, accompanied by his large family and his servants.

On his way back, a mysterious stranger appeared and started to wrestle with Jacob. This went on all night long. By daybreak, the stranger did not succeed in overcoming Jacob.

"Let me go, for the day breaketh!" pleaded the stranger.

"I will not let you go," said Jacob, "until you bless me."

"What is your name?" asked the stranger.

"Jacob," was the reply.

"Your name shall no longer be Jacob," said the stranger. "From now on you shall be called *Yisrael*."

From that time on, Jacob had a second name. In addition to Jacob, he was called Yisrael or Israel, meaning "one who struggles with God." This new name, Yisrael, was given to all descendants of Jacob. It also became the name of the homeland of the Jewish people — Eretz Yisrael—the land of Israel.

From One Tribe to Twelve

Jacob was the father of 12 sons and one daughter.. Since Jacob was also known by the name Israel, his sons were called Children of Israel—or, in Hebrew, *Bnai Yisrael*. In later years *all* Jews were called Children of Israel.

As the Children of Israel increased in numbers they formed tribes. The tribes were named after the sons (and some grandsons) of Jacob. The names of the sons of Jacob are mentioned in the last chapters of the Book of Genesis. They include: Reuben, Simeon, Levi, Judah, Zebulun, Issachar, Dan, Gad, Asher, Naphtali, Joseph and Benjamin. The name of his daughter was Dinah.

Of Jacob's 12 sons, all became tribes *except* Levi and Joseph. The people who later served in the Temple were descendants of Levi and they served *all* the people, so they did not become a tribe. And Joseph did not become a tribe. Instead, his two sons, Manasseh and Ephraim, formed two separate tribes.

How the Tribes Kept United

Because of their constant wanderings, the members of the tribes intermingled with the Canaanites. As a result, some of the Children of Israel forgot about their brit with God. However, most of the members of the various tribes remained loyal to the covenant.

One of the practices that helped keep the tribes together was the assembly they attended every year in the springtime. This was the time when the grass was green and the water was plentiful. Together, the Children of Israel offered sacrifices and prayers to God.

At spring reunions, and at tribal meetings held around campfires during the rest of the year, elders told stories of how God created the world, made Adam and Eve, and placed them in the Garden of Eden. They told tales of a great flood that destroyed the wicked people but spared the righteous Noah and his family.

They loved best to tell and retell how Abraham got to know God, and how He made a covenant with him. Like Abraham, they wanted to be loyal to the covenant. They believed that God would treat them as He had promised Abraham.

These stories were never forgotton. For centuries our ancestors told them to their children. Now, we read them in our Tanach. Some scholars think that this spring festival was the earliest form of the great Jewish feast of *Pesach* (Passover), which we observe to this day.

The longer the Jews lived in Eretz Yisrael, the more they loved it, and the happier they were. Yet, as our next chapter will tell, they left the land promised them by God and they settled in Egypt.

Why did our ancestors move from Eretz Yisrael to Egypt?

CHAPTER 3

THE FIRST PESACH

In the northeast corner of Africa, with its northern border touching the Mediterranean Sea, and its eastern edge on the Red Sea, lies the land of Egypt. Its area is many times larger than Israel. Through the center of Egypt flows the great Nile River.

The waters of the Nile make the soil near both its banks fertile, but most of the rest of the land of Egypt is desert. More than 30 million people live in Egypt today. Although it is almost 400,000 square miles in area, most of the population is crowded into the cities, villages, and farm settlements within a few miles of the Nile. The language of Egypt today is Arabic, and the people call themselves Arabs. They are, however, a mixture of many peoples including, ancient Egyptians, Africans, Greeks, Romans, Europeans and others.

The Egyptians: 3,500 Years Ago

When the Jews came to Egypt 3,500 years ago, the country was already very old. For a long time before that, it was ruled by leaders whose title was "Pharaoh." The Pharaohs were not satisfied to rule *only* their own country. With their large armies, they controlled and taxed many cities in Eretz Yisrael as well as cities and villages in other countries that lay close to their borders.

Many Egyptians were educated, and many were skilled at various types of work. Among them were architects, engineers, doctors, musicians, writers and poets. They succeeded in building great and beautiful temples, large and comfortable palaces, and even the huge pyramids for which the land is famous, and which still stand to this day.

The pyramids served as burial places for the Pharaohs and the members of their families. The dead bodies were treated with chemicals and then bound in sheets. After this careful preparation, the bodies were laid in expensive caskets. The caskets were then placed in sealed chambers in the pyramids. Some of these bodies, called *mummies,* were found thousands of years later, and may still be seen in museums.

The ancient Egyptians kept records by carving pictures and writings in stone, and also by writing on rolls of *papyrus* — which is like strong, heavy paper. These records tell us that rich Egyptians wore beautiful garments, lived in comfortably furnished homes, rode in chariots drawn by horses, and traveled up and down the Nile in swift sailing ships which were propelled by many oarsmen.

Most of the Egyptians in the times of the Pharaohs, however, were very poor. Some were nomads who spent their lives wandering in the desert. Those who lived in the cities were poor and had no education. They lived in tiny, uncomfortable brick houses.

The farmers were somewhat better off, especially in those years when the Nile River rose enough to water their lands. When the water of the Nile was plentiful, some was channeled off to more distant fields. As a result, these too yielded rich harvests. If the waters did not rise, many crops would fail and many people would die of hunger.

How the Jews Came to Egypt

During their first centuries in Eretz Yisrael, the Jews had become very attached to their land. This was during the time when Jacob's family was growing up. But, like in Egypt, there were times when so little rain fell that many of their sheep and cattle died of thirst, and many people went hungry.

One year the drought (dry spell) was very serious. It lasted for a long time and Jews were afraid that their families might starve. Fortunately, passing travelers reported that though the famine was bad everywhere, the drought did not seriously damage the grass in Egypt, and food could be purchased there.

Knowing of no other way of saving themselves, many Jews left their land, Eretz Yisrael, and—about 3,500 years ago—made their way to Egypt where they settled in an area known as Goshen.

Our Tanach tells the story of this migration of Jews to Egypt somewhat differently. It tells us that Joseph, son of the patriarch, Jacob, was sold as a slave to an Egyptian nobleman. Joseph's wisdom helped him win his freedom. He was given a position in the government second only to that of the Pharaoh. During the famine in Eretz Yisrael, Joseph brought his father and his family to Egypt. He settled them in the fertile region called Goshen.

How the Jews Became Slaves

For some years all went well in Egypt, and the Jews remained in Goshen. But, a century or more later, a cruel Pharaoh took away the freedom of the Jews, as well as the freedom of others who were not native Egyptians.

They became slaves.

Under the eyes of guards carrying whips and clubs, the slaves worked hard making bricks, hauling huge building blocks, and laying them in place. When a slave became tired, he was beaten. Often he died. Work began at sunrise, and continued until sundown, and often late into the night. This was the type of slave-labor used to build many of the pyramids.

The Jews often thought about the stories which their fathers and grandfathers had told. They remembered especially God's brit with Abraham, and His promise to protect the Jewish people and give them Eretz Yisrael. They hoped that God would make good His promise, and would take them out of their slavery in Egypt, and would lead them in freedom to Eretz Yisrael.

Years passed without a hopeful sign. Many lost courage and were satisfied living in slavery. They became human machines: working, eating, sleeping—with nothing to hope for.

A Freedom-Leader Is Born

One day a man named Moses appeared among the Jews and brought them startling news. "God," he said, "the God who made a brit with our father Abraham, the God who we, Bnai Yisrael, worship, has decided to set His people free!"

Few believed him, but they did begin to wonder about this man Moses. Soon, they began hearing strange and wonderful tales about him. He was the son of a Jewish man named Amram and a Jewish woman named Jochebed. When Moses was born, the Pharaoh of Egypt issued an edict that all sons of Hebrew slaves be drowned in the Nile River. He found that too many Jewish babies were being born and this worried him.

To save his life, when Moses was three months old, his parents set him on the banks of the Nile in a watertight basket. There, a princess found him and adopted him as her own son.

As an Egyptian prince, Moses received a good education and enjoyed the life of luxury in the king's palace. One day, he discovered that he was really a Jew, and he decided to learn more about his people. He looked for them and found them among the slaves.

Moses was filled with pity for his brother-Jews. When he saw a Jewish slave beaten, he became so enraged that he killed the cruel Egyptian. Moses then fled into the desert—to the land of Midian—and there he became a shepherd.

Moses Makes a Discovery

While tending his flock deep in the wilderness near Mount Sinai, Moses saw a wonderful sight: A bush was in flames, yet, it did not burn up! As Moses stood wondering, he heard a voice saying:

> I am the God of your fathers. I have a covenant with your people—the Jews. I have seen their suffering in Egypt, and I have decided to set them free. I, hereby, appoint you, Moses, to be My messenger. I will help you set My people free.

Nowadays, we rarely hear of visions such as Moses saw.

Did Moses really see a burning bush?
Did he hear God?

We will really never know. And, actually, it does not matter. The fact is that Moses had been thinking for a long time of a way to free the Jews from their slavery. Now, after his wonderful experience, he felt sure that he would succeed.

Moses returned to Egypt. He appeared before the Pharaoh, and said, "The God of the Jewish people commands: 'Let My people go!'" Naturally, the Pharaoh laughed. He thought of Moses as nothing more than a madman.

Moses did not have much success with the Jewish slaves either. When he announced that God would free them from slavery, they paid no attention. They were too hungry and tired to think seriously about anything—except how to get food and rest, and how to avoid the whip of the guard.

Freedom Finally Comes

But, then, after a series of troubles suddenly befell Egypt, Pharaoh began to take Moses more seriously! Jews, too, who until then had paid little attention to Moses, began to believe that their God was helping them.

The Bible describes how 10 terrible plagues struck the Egyptians. First, the waters of the Nile turned to blood. Then, grasshoppers covered the land and ruined the crops. The plague of lice, and the plague of wild beasts, and other plagues followed one after the other. When the tenth plague arrived, and Pharaoh found that his oldest son had died, he let the Jewish slaves leave Egypt.

There was little time for the Jews to prepare. Hastily they packed their belongings and fled toward the Sinai desert. They believed they were free at long last, and they were filled with joy as they followed Moses.

An oasis in the heart of the Sinai Desert.

But their happiness did not last long. On the seventh day after their escape, they found themselves in front of the Sea of Reeds (once thought to be the Red Sea). This is a body of water which we believe is now a part of the Suez Canal. While searching for a way to reach the other side of the water safely, they discovered that armed Egyptian soldiers were pursuing them. The Jews knew, immediately, what this meant. The Egyptians had changed their minds. They wanted to bring them back to a life of slavery in Egypt.

Miracle at the Sea

The Jews became frantic. They had no army with which to fight the Egyptians, and they knew of no way to get across the Sea of Reeds.

Moses, however, remained calm. He felt confident that God would save His people, and he prayed hard.

Suddenly, the Egyptians were very close. However, as darkness fell, they were forced to stop the pursuit and to rest for the night. The next morning, the Egyptians could no longer find the Jews. They were safely across the Sea of Reeds.

Just how they managed their escape, we do not know. Our ancestors were certain that God had done this for them. In the Bible, the crossing is described very dramatically. During the night, it says, a strong wind blew over the sea. In the morning, Moses found the waters so low that he could lead his people safely across.

As the Jews crossed, they looked at the water on either side, and it appeared to stand motionless, like walls! By the time the Egyptians awoke, the Jews were well on their way.

Quickly, the Egyptian soldiers mounted their horses and chariots, and pursued the Jews into the valley that was once a sea. But horses and chariots are heavy, and the mud was thick. Soon, all the Egyptian horses and riders were stuck in the mud. The waters of the sea then returned to normal, and the Egyptian army was drowned.

Sing a Song of Thanks

The Jews were now safe! Moses had spoken the truth! God had saved them as He had promised their ancestors, the patriarchs. He kept His promise made to Abraham,

Isaac and Jacob! God was their Protector! God was mighty, mightier than anyone on earth or in heaven! Led by Miriam, the sister of Moses, the Children of Israel danced and sang:

Who is like you, O Lord!
Who is like You?

The escape from Egypt was such an important and exciting event that the Children of Israel decided never to let their descendants forget it. More than 3,200 years have passed since we were freed from Egyptian slavery, yet we continue to celebrate a feast called *Pesach* (Passover) in honor of the great deliverance. Each year at Pesach (usually during the month of April), Jewish families hold a service in the home called the *Seder*. During the Seder, we read from the *haggadah* which tells the story of the exodus from Egypt. Children are encouraged to ask questions about Pesach, and their elders answer them. Unleavened bread (*matzah*) is eaten, and even the very young drink wine that night!

During the Seder, we sing a song that says if God had *only* saved us from Egypt, and had helped us in *no other* way—it would have been enough—*dayenu*! (Dayenu is a Hebrew word meaning, "It would have been enough.")

In our next chapter, we shall learn that God, continuing to use Moses as His messenger, did much more for our ancestors. Let's find out about it!

CHAPTER 4

HOW OUR ANCESTORS
LEARNED TO BE FREE

The First Freedom Holiday

Young Jews today, after many years of study, ascend a beautifully decorated pulpit and solemnly promise to continue living as faithful Jews. This ceremony, which is called Confirmation, is conducted in many congregations in the United States and in other countries.

The celebration is held on *Shavuot*. Shavuot is also known as the Feast of Weeks or Pentecost. Our Tanach tells us that the first confirmation ceremony took place on Shavuot. It was so dramatic an event that our ancestors never forgot it!

Are We Free If We Are Not Slaves?

The first confirmands were all the Jews whom Moses had led out of the slavery of Egypt. They felt free. They no longer had to work long hours every day. They no longer had to obey Egyptian overseers who lashed them, and made them feel like animals.

Our ancestors, however, were not *really* free. Moses, their leader, noticed it and said that they *acted* like slaves, even though they were no longer in Egypt.

Our Tanach relates many incidents that illustrate this.

Shortly after their escape from Egypt, the people stopped for water. They were disappointed when they found it too bitter to drink. Instead of searching for other water, or for ways to improve it, they all ran to Moses and complained. He found a way to sweeten it.

Another time, they were again without water. Again, and again they ran to Moses and complained bitterly. This time, he found water for them by striking a rock!

When the food the Children of Israel carried with them from Egypt was gone, they ran to Moses complaining that they were hungry. He taught them how to find a new type of food which they called *manna.*

Once, when a great flock of birds descended upon their camp, they snared them and ate them so greedily that many became sick, and some even died.

Why Some Free People Are Still Slaves

Moses was patient with his people because he understood the reasons for their behavior. He knew why they could not think or act for themselves. In Egypt, they had had to depend on the overseers or guards for everything. They had never learned to plan for the future, because the Egyptian overseers did all the planning. They had never learned to be responsible people, because the Egyptian overseers had never given their slaves any responsibility.

Moses was wise enough to realize that the Jews he had led out of Egypt needed help. They had to be taught to rely upon themselves, rather than on him or any other leader. Therefore, he decided to teach his people to know more about God.

Moses thought back to his younger years when he lived in the desert. He remembered the bush that kept on burning, but was never burnt up. He was only a shepherd then tending the sheep of his father-in-law, Jethro. He recalled hearing the voice of God speaking to him, telling him not to go near the bush, for it was on holy ground.

Moses decided that it was to that holy spot, deep in the desert, near Mount Sinai, that he wanted to lead the Children of Israel. It was on that holy ground that Moses decided to teach the Children of Israel about God.

The Great Mountain in the Desert

At Mount Sinai, our forefathers had their greatest experience since the crossing at the Sea of Reeds. Our Tanach relates that one day, shortly after their arrival, Mount Sinai suddenly began to quake. There was a tremendous roar. Flashes of flame shot through the sky. At that very moment, the Jews also heard a sound which they felt was the voice of God.

Filled with terror, they asked Moses for an explanation. He told them that God — the same God who had made a brit with Abraham, Isaac and Jacob, and Who had delivered them from slavery in Egypt, and Who had saved them at the Sea of Reeds, and Who had provided for their needs while they were wandering in the wilderness — that God had now come to renew the brit with them. God, Moses added, would make them His chosen people and would continue to protect them *if*—if they promised to obey Him and to teach their children to do so.

The Ten Commandments

When the people asked Moses exactly what God expected of them, he said in God's name: These are ten things God wants you to believe in and to do:

1. You must believe that I am the one and only God. I delivered you out of the slavery of Egypt and made you free.
2. You must not believe in any other gods or idols, and you must not pray to them.
3. You must respect My name by speaking only the truth.
4. You must observe the Sabbath (*Shabbat*) as a holy day. It is a special day to remind you that I created the world and set you free.
5. You must respect your parents.
6. You must not murder.
7. You must not be immoral.
8. You must not steal.
9. You must be fair and honest in dealing with your fellow man.
10. You must not desire things that don't belong to you, and which you have no right to have.

These are the Ten Commandments.

But there are many more commandments God expects the Jewish people to obey. He expects us to treat all human beings, and even animals, in a kindly way. He expects us to be helpful to those who are poor, or sick, or cannot take care of themselves. He expects us to assist strangers so that even they will feel wanted and safe living among us.

These and many other commandments were laid before the people.

The people listened respectfully as Moses spoke in God's name. When Moses finished speaking, they cried out:

> We shall perform the *mitzvot* (commandments) and continue to learn God's teachings, so that we can carry them out more perfectly.

We, today, agree! For this reason we include in our prayers the famous proclamation:

HEAR, O ISRAEL, THE LORD OUR GOD, THE LORD IS ONE!

Moses was pleased to tell God that the Jewish people still accepted the covenant that He first made with Abraham. Then, Moses offered a sacrifice, which was his way of confirming the brit between God and the Jewish people. And, every year, in many congregations, at Shavuot-time that agreement is re-confirmed through the Confirmation ceremony.

Because Shavuot is so closely related to the receiving of the Ten Commandments at Mount Sinai, it is also known by the name *Zeman Matan Toratenu*. These three Hebrew words mean, "the time when our Torah was given to us." But Shavuot *really* means "weeks"—the

Festival of Weeks, for it takes place seven weeks after the first day of the Passover holiday.

The Golden Calf

The Tanach tells us that after preparing the people for a few days at the foot of Mount Sinai, Moses went up to the top of the mountain. After 40 days, he returned with a pair of stone tablets. The Ten Commandments were carved on them. It was to be a reminder that the people must always remember their brit with God.

But, as Moses came closer to the camp, he beheld a terrible sight! The people, who had just promised to worship God alone, were worshiping a golden idol in the shape of a calf! Moses saw it and was angry. He threw the tablets to the ground and smashed them. Then, he rushed into the crowd and reprimanded them for not keeping their promise. As he did this, he destroyed the idol that they had made.

Promises Are Not Enough

Moses now knew that promises were not enough to make a weak people strong or free. They had to be *taught* to love freedom and to obey the commandments. He, therefore, prepared a second pair of tablets and placed them in a beautiful chest called the Holy Ark. We still use the same name for the ark on the synagogue pulpit. Today, the ark contains the Torah scrolls.

Moses then placed the ark in a special tent and appointed the men of the tribe of Levi to take care of it. He also appointed his brother, Aaron, and Aaron's family to act as priests (as *Kohanim*, as they are called in Hebrew), and to conduct worship services and to offer sacrifices.

Our Ancestors Learn Slowly

The tablets, the ark, the sacred tent, the levites and the priests were constant reminders to the people of their covenant with God. And, little by little, the Jewish people learned to know what God expected of them.

Santa Katarina, a Greek Orthodox monastery built at the foot of what some believe to be Mount Sinai, where Moses received the Ten Commandments.

From time to time, Moses would become disappointed when he saw how long it took the people to learn. Once, after years of marching through the desert on the way to the Promised Land (or Eretz Yisrael as we have been calling it), the Children of Israel came close to its southern border. Moses sent out 12 scouts to look over the land which God had promised to give them. Upon their return, 10 scouts reported that the country was good and fertile, but that the inhabitants were very strong, and would not let the Jews enter. Only two scouts — one, whose name was Joshua, and the other whose name was Caleb—felt the Jews could overcome the enemy. But the majority insisted that if a fight occurred, the Jews would be defeated.

The report frightened the people, and Moses realized that, despite the covenant, they did not yet have enough faith in God and in themselves.

Moses Continues to Teach

Moses decided to train his people, and to strengthen their confidence in God and in themselves. To gain time, he delayed their stay in the desert before trying to enter the Promised Land. During those years of wandering through the Sinai desert, Moses taught them to face the dangers of the desert: heat, cold, hunger, thirst, wild beasts, poisonous creatures, and occasional attacks by enemy tribes.

With the help of his assistant, Joshua, Moses organized the Jews into an army by tribes. As the years went by, the old and weak men and women gradually died out, and those who had a slave mentality disappeared. The young generation of Jews that grew up in the desert learned to believe in God and to rely on themselves. After many years — our Tanach says, 40 years — Moses felt the Jews were really free and prepared to enter Eretz Yisrael.

Moses then led his people out of the Sinai desert and proceeded northward along the eastern side of the Jordan River. There, they met up with enemies who tried to block their way. By now, however, the Jews were no longer afraid. They had become self-reliant and confident of God's help.

Led by Joshua, the tribes defeated their enemies, and took possession of a great stretch of land on the eastern side of the Jordan. Boldly, they prepared to cross to the western side, to the Promised Land. (At this time, the Promised Land was called Canaan. Later it was renamed Eretz Yisrael, and still later Palestine.)

The Feast of Sukkot

Moses now knew that he had succeeded. He had taught his people to accept responsibility. They were a people that believed in God, and they wanted to keep the brit that Abraham first made with Him.

Realizing that his death was near, Moses urged his fellow Jews to enter Eretz Yisrael without fear. He reminded them that they owed thanks to God for having protected them while they were wandering in the wilderness. So that they would not forget those difficult years in the desert, they agreed to observe a new festival. It was called *Sukkot*, meaning, Feast of Booths.

To this day, in the fall of the year, when the weather turns chilly, many Jews still erect a *sukkah*. It has four walls and a roof made of the branches of trees. Dwelling in a sukkah (booth) is a reminder of the dangers and discomforts of the desert which our ancestors lived through. Though it is difficult for many of us to erect our own sukkah, we do visit sukkot (sukkot is the plural of sukkah) built by our synagogues. Those who do have their own sukkah usually eat their meals in it during the week of Sukkot. Some even sleep in it.

Moses Does Not Enter the Land

Moses, the faithful servant of God, and the greatest of our leaders, never entered Eretz Yisrael. He died on a mountain overlooking the Promised Land.

Jews never forgot Moses. He stands out as the greatest leader of all time, as God's spokesman, and as our greatest teacher. We call him *Moshe Rabbenu* (Moses Our Teacher), and we believe no one ever lived who was his equal.

Jewish tradition proclaims Moses as the first and greatest prophet!

These are the remains of a theater built in Roman times in Beit Shean — one of the first towns in Eretz Yisrael. Beit Shean is located about 40 miles from Haifa and dates back about 6,000 years.

SUMMARY OF UNIT I

The covenant or brit between God and our ancestors was the most important event in our history. The brit was the beginning of Jewish life. Because of the brit, the religion of the Jewish people differs from that of our neighbors. To fulfill the covenant, the Jewish people came to Eretz Yisrael in the days of Abraham.

When famine struck their land, some tribes moved to Egypt. There, a cruel Pharaoh enslaved them. Moses freed our ancestors from Egyptian bondage, and led them safely across the Sea of Reeds.

At the foot of Mount Sinai, Bnai Yisrael (the Children of Israel) became a united people. There, they renewed Abraham's brit with God. They promised to obey God's *mitzvot* (commandments), among which were the Ten Commandments. Through this first confirmation ceremony in history, the Jews proved that they wanted to be the "covenant people" and to follow the brit first made between God and Abraham.

Our ancestors, despite their promise, did not always remain faithful to the brit. Shortly after they promised to obey the mitzvot, they bowed before a golden calf!

In time, the Jews were led by Moses and Joshua to the border of Eretz Yisrael.

We celebrate Pesach to remind us that God, ever faithful to the brit, saved our people from slavery. We observe Shavuot to remind us of the confirmation of the covenant with God at Mount Sinai. We erect a sukkah on Sukkot in thanksgiving to God for being faithful to the brit and for protecting our ancestors during years of great danger.

Introduction

THE JEWISH PEOPLE BECOMES A NATION

Israel is an independent nation today. Unlike other nations, however, its special day of rest is Shabbat. Its public schools teach the Hebrew Tanach and the Jewish way of life along with the same kind of subjects that you study in your public school. Its language is Hebrew. Israel is a modern Jewish nation that came into being in 1948.

Although Israel is a very *new* nation, it is also a very *old* nation. It was first established about 3,000 years ago. This was 200 years after the Jews were led out of Egypt by Moses and into the Promised Land by Joshua.

The Jews living at that time were members of different tribes, and each tribe was governed by its own leader. There was no central government or organization that held *all* the tribes together. No person had the power to make all the people follow his instructions.

42

3000 YEARS AGO SAMUEL, THE LAST JUDGE, APPOINTED SAUL TO BE KING OF ALL THE TRIBES.

KING DAVID FOUGHT MANY ENEMIES AND MADE THE KINGDOM STRONGER AND LARGER.

KING SOLOMON KEPT THE KINGDOM UNITED AND BUILT THE TEMPLE IN JERUSALEM.

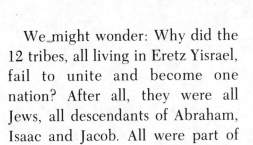

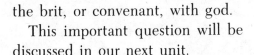

2900 YEARS AGO THE KINGDOM DIVIDED INTO TWO— ISRAEL AND JUDAH.

TODAY—YOU AND I AND OTHER JEWS LIVE IN MANY LANDS.

We might wonder: Why did the 12 tribes, all living in Eretz Yisrael, fail to unite and become one nation? After all, they were all Jews, all descendants of Abraham, Isaac and Jacob. All were part of the brit, or convenant, with god.

This important question will be discussed in our next unit.

3 MILLION JEWS NOW LIVE IN THE OLD-NEW NATION OF ISRAEL.

An ancient temple located in Arad, about 25 miles from Beer Sheba. The stones in the center are altars. The Jews in the days of Moses tried to enter the Promised Land at this point but were beaten back by Canaanite tribes.

CHAPTER 5

THE JEWISH TRIBES RETURN
TO ERETZ YISRAEL

Today, almost all the people of the world are divided into nations. Some are large like the United States, Russia and China. Many are small like Israel, Lebanon and Cyprus. Often, nations go to war with one another.

To promote peace, over 100 nations joined the United Nations. They erected a beautiful 39 story building in New York City, and they meet there regularly to seek ways to prevent wars and maintain peace.

Canaan in the Days of Moses and Joshua

In the days of Moses and Joshua, 3,200 years ago, there were no nations as we know them today. In fact, very few nations existed at all. Most people were members of small tribes who often were busy fighting each other.

Eretz Yisrael, which at that time was still called Canaan, was a land in which many different peoples and tribes made their home. The largest group was the Canaanites.

Taking possession of Eretz Yisrael once again was not easy for the Jews. Since the times when Abraham, Isaac and Jacob lived there, the number of Canaanites had increased greatly. They occupied most of the land that had formerly been vacant.

They did not welcome the *Hebrews* who had been slaves in Egypt and were now returning. And so, to re-enter Eretz Yisrael, the Jews were forced to fight their way back.

The Canaanites were well armed. They had sharp metal weapons—swords, spears, axes, and arrows—and some of their warriors wore armor to protect them. The Jews had few of these instruments of war. Some had only slings to hurl stones, and others made weapons out of sharp stones.

Fighting on level ground was especially dangerous for the Jews, because the Canaanites had chariots in which they could move more swiftly than foot-soldiers. They also had large shields which protected them.

It was very difficult for the Jews to conquer the Canaanite cities, because their thick walls made it impossible to break through. And yet, it is a fact that under the leaderhip of Joshua, the Jews *did* reconquer much of Eretz Yisrael.

Joshua's Success

Why was Joshua so successful in his campaign to conquer Eretz Yisrael? Our Tanach gives two accounts of the war. One report claims that God was responsible for the victories; that many miracles and unusual happenings helped Joshua. For example:

1. God stopped the flow of the Jordan River to enable the Jews to cross from the eastern to the western bank.

2. God caused the huge walls of Jericho to collapse so that they could enter the city and destroy it.
3. God told Joshua how to capture a city called Ai by a clever scheme.
4. God sent a heavy hailstorm to confuse the army of one enemy.
5. God made the sun stand still so the day would be longer and the army could complete the attack against the enemy.

With God's support, according to this account, Joshua was able to conquer all 31 kings who had ruled the land, and Eretz Yisrael once again became a Jewish country. The only Canaanites Joshua did not have to conquer by force were the Gibeonites. They surrendered without a fight.

The second account is somewhat different. It tells us that Joshua did not have to fight to conquer all the territory, because he received help from some members of the native population.

How was this possible? Who were the people who would have helped Joshua?

Archeologists have dug up interesting evidence to prove that not *all* Jews were slaves in Egypt. According to this theory, when Jacob's family went to Egypt at the invitation of Joseph, many Jews stayed behind and *never left* the land of Canaan. It was these Jews who lived there all along, and had never been slaves in Egypt, who helped Joshua conquer parts of Canaan.

How the Land Was Divided

Settling down in Eretz Yisrael was certainly not easy for our ancestors. They were not yet united into a nation. While most tribes followed the leadership of Joshua, there were times when one tribe or another went off to live by itself.

Naturally, the Jews had to fight long and hard for every inch of ground. They had to endure many hardships. They did not enjoy fighting. They fought only because they firmly believed that God wanted them to do so. This was the agreement, this was the covenant that God made with the Jews way back in the days of Abraham.

In the course of time, the tribe of Judah made its home in the area south of Jerusalem. But Jerusalem was strongly fortified, and it remained in the hands of the Canaanites for centuries. Two smaller tribes, Simeon and Dan settled nearby.

To the north of Jerusalem, in the central part of Eretz Yisrael, the powerful tribe of Ephraim established itself. The tribes of Manasseh and Benjamin settled down next to Ephraim.

To the north of these tribes lay the most fertile valley in Eretz Yisrael—the Valley of Jezreel. This valley, like Jerusalem, was strongly fortified and most of the time remained in the hands of the Canaanites.

North of Jezreel, the tribes of Asher, Zebulun, Naphtali and Issachar were given a large area in which to settle.

A fourth group, consisting of the tribes, Reuben, Gad, and part of the tribe of Manasseh, occupied the eastern side of the Jordan.

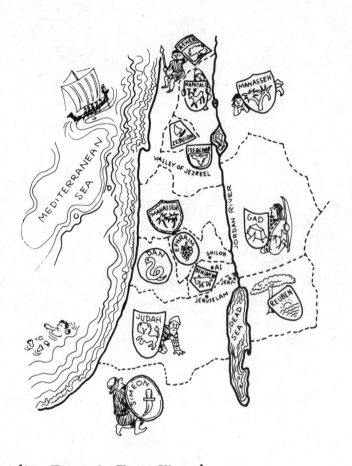

Settling Down in Eretz Yisrael

After settling in Eretz Yisrael, the Jews did not immediately organize themselves into a nation. Instead, each tribe looked to its own tribal leader for guidance and protection.

There were many reasons why it would have been proper for the tribes to unite:

    1. They were all members of the Children of Israel, bound by a brit with God and obliged to worship Him.

2. All of them, even those whose ancestors had not been slaves in Egypt, learned about Moses. They had heard about the marvelous redemption from Egyptian slavery. They felt that God had saved *them* as well as their fellow Jews.
3. They all believed that God had fulfilled His promise, and that He had helped them get possession of Eretz Yisrael.

Why, then, did they *not* organize themselves into a nation?

1. As far back as the Jews could remember, they had always been members of tribes. They were friendly to one another. Yet, no single leader ever arose after the patriarchs who was able to hold the tribes together.
2. Groups of tribes were separated from one another by Canaanite cities and fortresses, and communication between the tribes was poor.
3. No schools existed for teaching the young their responsibilities to God and to their fellow Jews. Fathers were expected to perform this duty. Some fathers did, but many did not.

Jews Learn from Canaanites

When the Jews settled in their new homes in Eretz Yisrael, those who lived north of Jerusalem, and many who lived in Judah to the south, discovered that the surest way to earn a living was to raise grain, vegetables, olives, grapes and other fruits. Most of them had been shepherds and did not know how to farm. They needed to learn, and the best teachers were the Canaanites.

Canaanite farmers taught Jews how to plow, sow, care for plants, and reap the produce of the soil. At the same time, the Canaanites insisted that to keep the land fertile one had to win the favor of Baal. Baal was the name of the favorite god of the Canaanites. Only Baal, the Canaanite farmers believed, could make the earth fertile.

Jews Begin to Worship Baal

Since there were no schools, many Jews did not realize that they must worship God *alone*. They did not consider it wrong to worship Baal as well as God, so they brought offerings to Baal. The result was that many Jews gradually stopped worshiping God, and they forgot their obligation to live up to the covenant, to the brit.

How strange! After all the years of yearning and struggle to settle in Eretz Yisrael and live as God's chosen people, the Jews were slowly forgetting God, the brit, and their responsibilities as Jews! The Jewish people was beginning to fall apart!

Fortunately, however, things began to happen that slowed down this dangerous trend. Our next chapter will tell us what happened.

CHAPTER 6

THE TRIBES FACE A CHALLENGE

For hundreds of years, Eretz Yisrael was called Palestine. It was the Romans who created this name about 1,800 years ago.

But why did the Romans decide to use this name? Why did they decide to call Eretz Yisrael, which means the Land of Israel, Palestine, which means the Land of the Philistines?

Who were the Philistines? We shall find out about them in this chapter.

Jewish Tribes Attacked

In our last chapter, we learned that the Jews who came to Eretz Yisrael in the days of Joshua were divided into tribes. Because they were not united under one central government, many enemies attacked, robbed, and killed them. Moabites, Ammonites, and Arameans came from the eastern side of the Jordan, and attacked the Jewish tribes. Midianites from Arabia, and Amalekites from the Negev, which lay to the south of Judah, raided Jewish villages and farms. They carried off the crops of the field. They terrorized and murdered many people.

More dangerous than the enemies *surrounding* Eretz Yisrael were the unconquered Canaanites *inside* the country. They posed a double threat.

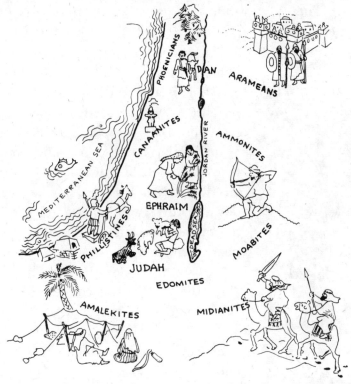

First, many Jews began to worship the idols of the Canaanites and gave up the worship of God. This hurt the unity of the Jewish people.

Second, the Canaanite people had good armies. They kept attacking the tribes of Israel. The attacks were well planned. Had the Jews then been united as a nation, with *one* army, they might have been able to defend the individual tribes. Being divided, however, the enemy was able to pick off one tribe at a time. Few tribes took the trouble to assist any of the others.

Judges Save the Tribes

How did the tribes save themselves? Each time a tribe was under heavy attack, a leader, called a *judge,* would arise. The judge would raise a local army and drive off the enemy.

One excellent judge was a woman named Deborah. She lived about 3,100 years ago, and was famous as a prophet as well as a judge. Once, she learned that the Canaanites had assembled a large army, and were ready to attack. She turned for help to *all* the Jewish tribes. They let her down. Only six out of the 12 tribes responded, sending a total of 10,000 poorly-armed men.

Deborah was disappointed. Nevertheless, she was convinced that God would help His chosen people, and she appointed Barak, whose name means "lightning," to command the army.

Deborah's confidence in God and Barak was soon justified. The Canaanites, equipped with chariots and armor, gathered in the Valley of Jezreel near a brook. Barak stationed his men on a hill not far off. A heavy downpour made the valley muddy. The brook overflowed its banks and the Canaanite chariots were stuck in the mud. Like lightning, Barak struck the Canaanites, who had been slowed down by the mud, and destroyed their entire army. The victory was celebrated by a famous poem that we can still read in chapter five of the Book of Judges.

Philistines Threaten Eretz Yisrael

But this victory of Deborah and Barak was not enough to bring peace to Eretz Yisrael. A new enemy was arising on the western coast where the Philistines (a Greek people) lived. They had weapons and a military organization far superior to those of any other people in, or near, Eretz Yisrael. The Philistines forced the tribe of Dan, which lived close to them, to flee its territory and to search for new homes in the most northerly part of Eretz Yisrael.

Dan did not give up without a struggle. A judge named Samson appeared. According to the Tanach, Samson was so strong that he could take on and defeat a whole Philistine army! He was killed when he pushed apart the heavy, stone pillars of a huge Philistine temple. to which he was chained. The structure collapsed and fell on Samson and on the thousands of Philistines who were assembled nearby.

But no man alone—not even Samson—and no single tribe, could stop the Philistines. They conquered one tribe after the other. Soon, *all* the tribes were in danger.

Aware of the common danger, several tribes joined hands to battle the Philistines. But it was hopeless. The Philistines were too strong.

Then, the Jews tried to win God's help. From Shiloh, they brought the ark, in which were kept the Ten Commandment tablets. These were taken to the battlefield. But it did not help. The Philistines defeated them again. They captured the ark, and burned the city of Shiloh.

The destruction of Shiloh was a serious loss to the Jews. It was a holy place—a shrine—and served as a bond keeping the Jews united. As long as it existed, Jews from all tribes joined in caring for it. Now, with the loss of Shiloh, the tribes grew further apart.

But the defeat served one good purpose. It made the tribes realize that unless all 12 were united as a single nation, with a single leader, and with one army that included *all* their fighting men, the Philistines would soon take over *all* of Eretz Yisrael.

Samuel the Seer

There lived at that time—about 3,000 years ago—a man named Samuel. All the people respected him as a wise, religious leader. They called him Samuel the Seer because he could foresee future events. Some even believed that God revealed to him secrets unknown to any other man.

Fantastic stories about Samuel were spread over the land. His mother was Hannah. Hannah was unable to have a child for a long time. Finally, after much prayer, she gave birth to Samuel.

While still a child, Samuel became a priest in the city of Shiloh where a sanctuary had been built. Here, sacrifices were offered to God.

While in Shiloh, God revealed to him events that were to happen in the future. People found out about it and turned to him for help, and he always helped them.

In time, Samuel became a judge. He was different from any other judge who came before him. He was a man of peace. He never organized or led an army. Instead, he strengthened the feeling of unity among the Jews by:

1. Teaching them to live up to the brit;
2. Leading them in the worship of the One God;

3. Training young men, who became known as Sons of the Prophets, to go about the land, singing, dancing and praising God.

The Jews of Eretz Yisrael turned to Samuel the Seer to organize them into a nation.

What Samuel did in response to the people's request, and how the Jewish nation was finally established, we shall soon learn.

READ CHAPTER

CHAPTER 7

ONE NATION UNDER GOD

Needed: A Strong Leader

More than 2,000 years ago, our ancestors began to dream of a better world in which they would enjoy freedom, justice and peace. Relying on their brit with God, they expected that someday He would appoint a great and wise ruler who would guide them. They thought that this person would be someone like a king or a priest (a *kohen*), and that oil would be poured on his head. This would be the way of appointing him as leader. To pour oil on one's head meant to *anoint* him.

The good and wise leader to whom the Jews looked forward would be called the *Messiah*, which is a Hebrew word meaning "the anointed one." Jews always believed that the Messiah would be a descendant of King David.

Why Jews expected the Messiah to come from the family of David, we shall soon learn. First, let us find out what was happening among the tribes, and how things were going in the life-and-death struggle against the powerful Philistines—the enemy of the Jews.

58

Farmer Saul Becomes King Saul

Samuel the Seer hoped that teaching the Jews to be loyal to God and to the brit would be enough to keep them united. However, the Philistine victories over one tribe after the other, the destruction of Shiloh, and the capture of the ark convinced Samuel that a different way of uniting the tribes had to be found. Samuel realized that the only other way was to appoint a man whom all the tribes would accept as king.

Samuel was not happy about the idea of having a king. He knew that kings were likely to become proud and selfish. He feared they might oppress the very people they were suppose to help. Knowing of no quicker or better way to strengthen the people, he decided to take the step. He started the search for a man fit for leadership.

Samuel found a farmer by the name of Saul. Saul was a member of the tribe of Benjamin, and he seemed to have the necessary qualifications. He was young and brave; tall and handsome. At a great public ceremony, Samuel the Seer, with the approval of the tribal leaders, anointed Saul as king. The anointing was done by pouring holy oil on Saul's head. This signified that God was appointing him king. It also meant that he was responsible for his acts not only to the people, but also to God. The kingdom which Samuel started 3,000 years ago was to be a kingdom under God.

Saul Fails to Defeat the Philistines

King Saul made a good start. A report reached him that the Ammonites were attacking a Jewish city on the eastern side of the Jordan. He promptly sent messages to

Ashdod was one of the important cities that was a stronghold of the Philistines in the time of Samuel, Saul and David.

In the time of Samuel, before David slew the Philistine giant, Goliath, the Ark of the Lord was captured from the Israelites and carried off to Ashdod.

For many years, now, archeologists have been digging into the past of this ancient Philistine city. The ruins of ancient Ashdod contain layer upon layer of civilization from 1,300 B.C.E. to 500 B.C.E. Two trucks filled with oranges are about to be unloaded at the busy port of Ashdod in modern Israel.

all the tribes ordering them to send their fighting men. If any tribe failed to send warriors, it would face severe punishment. All tribes responded quickly. Though lightly armed, Saul's army overwhelmed the Ammonites.

Shortly thereafter, Saul's army defeated the Amalekites to the south. However, Saul could not defeat the major enemy—the Philistines.

Saul tried time and again to battle the powerful Philistines who had spread all over Eretz Yisrael. Once, Saul's son Jonathan won a victory. At other times, one of his captains, named David, led successful raids against the enemy. But at no time did Saul win a decisive victory.

Saul became discouraged and moody. Instead of paying attention to defeating the Philistines, he began to worry about Jonathan, his oldest son. He wanted Jonathan to be king after him. But David, Jonathan's close friend, was very popular. Saul was worried that David, rather that Jonathan, would become his successor. To keep David from the throne, Saul made up his mind to slay him.

Jonathan was a true friend, and he warned David of the king's plot. He also helped David escape.

King Saul had to fight hard against the Philistines. In a crucial battle on Mount Gilboa, near the Valley of Jezreel, the Philistines routed the Jews. Saul and Jonathan died in that battle, and the Philistine grip on Eretz Yisrael was now stronger than before.

Samuel Anoints David

Samuel the Seer died before the disaster on Mount Gilboa. But he foresaw what was going to happen, and he prepared for the future. Samuel realized that Saul was not the man who could unite the tribes. Although he was a brave and good man, he lacked the wisdom and skill to organize the people and to build a strong army.

While Saul was still alive, Samuel looked for another leader. He found him in David, son of Jesse. David and his family lived in Bethlehem, in the territory of Judah. At a secret ceremony, Samuel anointed David as the future king of the Jewish nation.

David never revealed the secret. He joined Saul's army and quickly became a captain. His fame grew, and he was admired for his bravery and his skill as a fighter. When Jonathan informed David that the king was jealous of him and planned to murder him, David fled and lived in hiding.

After the defeat on Mount Gilboa, and the death of Saul, the tribe of Judah announced that it wanted David to become king. But the northern tribes wanted a son of King Saul to be their king. After a few years of civil war, David was accepted as king over *all* the tribes, and the tribes of Israel were fully united as a nation.

David Does Wonders for the United Jewish Nation

David quickly proved that he was worthy of being anointed as king over the Jewish nation. He knew that one important job that he had to do was to free the nation from the Philistine enemy. David assembled all the fighting men, appointed officers who were courageous and experienced, and encouraged soldiers and officers to win promotions by acts of bravery.

With his army ready, David proceeded to unite his nation more firmly. The fortified city of Jerusalem, still in Canaanite hands, was a barrier separating the northern from the southern tribes. David decided to capture it. This, he knew, would be difficult. Jerusalem was situated on a steep hill and was protected by thick walls.

To the Canaanites, and to most Jews as well, it seemed that no force could possibly break into it. Once, the Canaanites boasted that the city was so well-protected that the lame and blind could defend it. However, David's men discovered a secret underground entrance

The walled-in Old City of Jerusalem as it looks
today. The dome in the center is the Mosque of
Omar.

to Jerusalem. Without opposition, they entered and captured the city. They then proclaimed it the capital of the
Jewish nation.

David's decision was wise and popular. Jerusalem had
never been the possession of any one particular tribe, so
now it belonged equally to *all* the Jews.

David established Jerusalem as the religious center for
all Jews. The holy ark containing the tablets of the law
(the Ten Commandments) was carried into Jerusalem.
With great pomp and ceremony, it was given a place of

honor near the king's palace. Priests (kohanim) were appointed, and the regular worship of God was resumed. From that time on, Jerusalem was known and loved as the holy city of the Jewish People.

David Conquers the Philistines

David was now ready to take on the Philistines. For many years they had oppressed the Jews, and David wanted to break their power. In a series of brilliant battles, he drove the Philistines out of Eretz Yisrael. This accomplishment was even more impressive than his previous achievements, and made him even more popular and beloved by the nation.

David had still more to give to his people. He conquered all the enemies that surrounded, and frequently attacked the Jews. He crossed to the eastern side of Jordan and conquered all the kingdoms bordering on Eretz Yisrael—the Edomites to the far south, the Moabites along the Dead Sea, the Ammonites by the Jordan, and the Arameans in the northeast. Under David, the Jewish nation grew larger and stronger than it had ever been.

David Wins the Love of the Jewish People

All this was not enough for David. He reorganized the government and the army. He appointed officials to govern and protect the people. He took a census, and this enabled him to know who was fit for service in the army, and who might best serve in other branches of the government. He established the nation on a strong foundation!

And this was not all! David was a wise judge, and he took personal charge of a court to which all the people were welcome to come if they felt unjustly treated. He was also a religious man; he respected God, prayed often, and composed many beautiful poems which he sang or recited.

Some of David's poems are still used in the worship services of both Jews and Christians. They are found in our Tanach in the Book of Psalms. All 150 psalms in the Book of Psalms are often called "the psalms of David," although he did not write all of them.

God's Promise to David

Our Tanach tells us that God made a special agreement with David! God promised him that his descendants would reign over the Jewish people forever.

No other Jewish king ever equalled David. Mindful of his truly great accomplishments and of the new, special covenant God made with him, it was natural for our ancestors to believe that the Messiah would be a member of David's family.

The accomplishments of King David were truly great. The Tanach and Talmud never tired of describing them.

Yet, all of David's achievements were not enough to keep the nation strong, prosperous, just and faithful to the brit with God. Many of his weaknesses and shortcomings showed up very quickly. Others took a bit longer to show themselves.

We shall learn of David's mistakes in the next chapter.

Relics of a private house at Meggido, built during the reign of King David.

CHAPTER 8

THE SEARCH FOR PEACE

About 75 years ago, Alfred Nobel, a wealthy Swedish industrialist, created the Nobel Foundation. Each year, since his death in 1896, five valuable prizes amounting to many thousands of dollars have been awarded to great men and women who have done outstanding work for the benefit of mankind.

One of the most important prizes is given to a person who does the most to promote peace. Some of the winners of this prize in the past were men like Albert Schweitzer, Ralph J. Bunche and Martin Luther King.

As we study the history of our people, we find that peace was a very important Jewish tradition as far back as the days of Abraham. Jews have always prayed for peace and worked for peace.

When David became king, he discovered that the northern and southern tribes were enemies. The tribe of Judah had been forced to fight a long war before the northern tribes accepted him (David) as king. David, therefore, decided that he would devote his life to keeping peace among his people—the people he loved.

How David United the Nation

In order to accomplish this goal, David worked hard to promote friendship among all Jews, regardless of the part of the country in which they lived. He did this in several ways:

1. He established Jerusalem as the capital because Jerusalem belonged equally to the northern and the southern tribes.
2. He made Jerusalem a holy city, and turned it into the religious center of the entire nation by bringing the ark there.
3. He appointed officials from both the north and the south, so that all parts of the country were represented in the government.
4. He set an example for the people by acting justly and being loyal to God.
5. He prepared well to fight off all enemies.

Even David Was Not Perfect

David had many wonderful qualities. Yet, like all human beings, he was less than perfect. Our Tanach tells us that David once fell in love with a married woman named Bathsheba. He wanted her to become his wife, and arranged to have her husband killed in battle. David was wrong, and a prophet named Nathan had the courage to tell it to him to his face! This was not the way a man who believes in God should act! Certainly, it was wrong for a king—a Jewish king—to act in this manner!

David realized that Nathan, the prophet—a messenger of God—was right. He humbly confessed that he had done wrong and prayed for forgiveness.

By admitting that he had done wrong, David set a good example for later Jewish kings. They learned to respect the prophets, about whom we shall study in our next unit. The kings who followed David rarely harmed the prophets, even when a prophet criticized them for doing wrong.

After ruling the nation for 40 years, David knew he would soon die. Several of his sons were ambitious and he feared they might fight for the throne. This would divide the people again. To prevent such a calamity, David decided to appoint his own successor, and he named his son, Solomon, to succeed him.

David's Tower, which stands in the old city of Jerusalem, was built in the days of King Herod.

Solomon Succeeds David

David's record in the area of peace did not satisfy the writers of our Tanach. They believed that he was involved in too many wars. He fought against too many of his fellow Jews to win the throne and to keep the throne. He also had made war with a great many of the enemies of the Jewish nation.

The authors of the Bible realized that David *had* to fight in order to establish peace in Eretz Yisrael. Nevertheless, they felt he had shed *too much* blood, and that he was not the right man to build a Temple. The Temple was to be a symbol of peace! And so, the task of building a Temple in which God could be worshiped was left to his son, Solomon. (Solomon is a name that means "peace" in Hebrew.)

Solomon the Wise

Solomon became king of Israel about 2,950 years ago. In many ways he proved to be a great king. Our Tanach called him "wise." To this day, a person who can solve difficult problems is called a Solomon.

Solomon showed his great wisdom particularly when he acted as a judge. The Tanach tells that he was once asked to decide which of two women was the mother of an infant child. Each mother claimed that the baby belonged to her.

Solomon ordered that a sword be brought to him. "I will cut the baby in half," he said to the quarreling mothers, "and will give half to each of you."

"No!" cried one of the women. "Don't hurt the baby. Give the baby to her!"

Immediately, Solomon realized that this was the real mother because she did not want her child harmed.

Solomon was also famous for his ability to solve all kinds of riddles. Once, the queen of the far-off land of Sheba (now called Yemen) made a journey to Jerusalem to test Solomon. One of these tests was very clever. It is described in the legends of the Jewish people that have come down to us through the ages.

The Queen of Sheba brought Solomon a bouquet of flowers. Each flower in the bunch looked and smelled alike. She challenged Solomon to separate the natural from the artificial flowers.

Solomon thought for a moment, then opened a window and allowed a bee to enter. By observing which flowers the bee was attracted to, Solomon immediately knew which were the natural flowers. Only real flowers contained honey.

In the Talmud, the rabbis state that Solomon understood *all* languages, even the languages of birds and beasts. So great was their admiration for Solomon that they claimed that he was the author of several books of the Bible including Proverbs, Ecclesiastes, and the Song of Songs.

Why Solomon Was Great

The accomplishments of King Solomon during his 40 years of rule over Israel are impressive:

Solomon Keeps Peace—Solomon succeeded in keeping peace for all the 40 years of his reign, and made peace agreements with the rulers of neighboring lands. Sometimes, as part of a treaty, he married the daughter or sisters of foreign kings. To discourage enemies from attacking his nation, he enlarged his army, strengthened the fortifications of many cities, and added horsemen and chariots to his fighting force.

Solomon Builds the Temple—A second accomplishment was the building of a beautiful Temple in Jerusalem. It was constructed of fine wood and stone. The inside contained many carvings, draperies and gold trimmings. There were golden candlesticks, and a small, gilded altar for burning incense, as well as a gold-covered table for the display of two loaves of bread symbolizing God's bounty.

At the back of the Temple was a simple room where only the holy ark was kept. Above the ark were two figures with outstretched wings. Aside from the caretakers, only the high priest (*kohen gadol*) was allowed to enter this chamber, which was called the Holy of Holies, and he did so only on Yom Kippur.

In the great courtyard surrounding the Temple, an altar was erected for sacrifices. A huge, bronze bowl served as a pool from which water was drawn for the use of the priests. The priests were expected to be clean in body and pure in spirit.

Jews from all parts of the land quickly learned to love the Temple. They visited it when they could, and flocked to it on each of the great festivals—Pesach, Shavuot and Sukkot. They worshiped God by bringing sacrifices which the priests offered with great ceremony. To add beauty to the Temple services, levites (members of the tribe of Levi) sang psalms to the accompaniment of musical instruments.

Coming to the Temple strengthened the Jews' devotion to God. It also helped to create better understanding among Jews. Being with fellow Jews from the north and the south, the east and the west, enabled them to become more friendly with one another and more concerned for each other.

Solomon Improves Culture—Solomon's third accomplishment was to raise the cultural level of his people. By appointing a large number of officials to keep all kinds of records, he encouraged many people to learn to read and write. Some men began to write wise sayings, stories, poems, and songs. Others wrote out parts of our Tanach which had, up to that time, been stored in people's memories, or had been written down only by a few. The process of writing down the stories and events in the life of our people continued for centuries.

Solomon Promotes Prosperity—Solomon's fourth contribution was to encourage his people to trade with foreign peoples as well as among themselves. Jews had never before engaged in business, but Solomon observed that Phoenicia (today called Lebanon), a land of small city-states near the northwestern border of Eretz Yisrael, was rich. It had become wealthy by trading with countries along the coast of the Mediterranean.

Solomon made friends with the Phoenician king, and hired skilled Phoenician workmen to help erect the Temple, and also to build ships for him. Solomon's fleet brought in valuable goods which enriched the country. Solomon also promoted overland trade by making it easier for caravans to come and go. Cities with large market places grew in Eretz Yisrael. Farmers and shepherds who found life in the country too difficult or unpleasant resettled in cities and became laborers.

Solomon Sows the Seeds of Strife

Solomon certainly did much to earn the love of his people. Yet, as our next chapter will tell, Solomon also sowed the poisonous seeds that led the nation to be split into two weak kingdoms!

Meggido—foundation of a gate built by King Solomon.

CHAPTER 9

STRIFE DIVIDES A NATION

A little more than 100 years ago, the terrible Civil War between the States brought misery and death to thousands upon thousands of Americans.

Within the last 25 years, two Asian countries, first Korea, then Vietnam, fought bitter wars between themselves—with brother killing brother.

In each case the problem was that the people of the northern part of each country could not agree with the people of the south about the form of government and the kind of laws under which all the population should live.

Solomon Brings Unhappy Times to Israel

When King Solomon died, about 2,900 years ago, the Jewish people faced a similar situation. The leaders of the 10 northern tribes could not agree with the southern tribes in Judah who should be king in place of Solomon. As a result, before long, the nation split into two parts.

Like his father, David, Solomon really wanted to strengthen the nation. But he failed because he was too proud. His pride led him to believe that he was the *master*, rather than the *servant* of his people. All this was proven after his death.

Solomon had not consulted anyone when he decided to marry foreign princesses. These marriages helped keep peace with the neighboring nations, but they stirred up bad feelings among the Jews. He also built elaborate houses for his foreign wives, and he even allowed them to worship their own gods.

Many Jews were angered by this idol worship, especially when it was practiced in Jerusalem. After all, the Temple was in Jerusalem, and Jerusalem was supposed to be a holy city for the *Jewish* people! To make matters worse, the people grew tired of the high taxes that they were forced to pay in order to support the palaces and mansions of the king.

To raise the vast sums of money needed for his ambitious enterprises, Solomon also had placed heavy taxes on the non-Jews whom David had conquered many years earlier. He made slaves of non-Jews living in Eretz Yisrael, and even forced Jews to work without pay for several months each year.

But all these measures did not bring in enough money to Solomon's treasury. Thoughts of revolt began to spread. Some people encouraged Jeroboam, a man who worked as a supervisor of Solomon's workers, to lead a rebellion. Solomon crushed it quickly, and Jeroboam had to flee for his life. There was no more talk of revolt in Solomon's lifetime.

The Temple Mount (Mt. Moriah). The First Temple was built here by Solomon. Still standing is the Western Wall of the Temple (at the bottom of the picture). The First Temple was destroyed in 586 B.C.E.

Differences Between South and North

The people of Judah remained loyal to Solomon for three reasons:

1. They believed that God had a special covenant with David promising that his descendants would always rule over them.
2. Jerusalem was close to them. On special occasions they visited the city, and they loved it. They loved their beautiful Temple, and they respected Solomon because he built it.
3. Many, perhaps most, of Solomon's officials were members of the tribe of Judah. Solomon came from the same tribe.

The Jews who lived in the north did not feel the same way about Solomon and the royal family. They were pleased with the Temple, but most of them lived too far away to visit it often. Also, the fact that so many government officials were southerners led the northerners to believe that Solomon was playing favorites. So, the Jews of the north were determined to revolt at the first opportunity. It came when Solomon died.

The Split Between Israel and Judah

Solomon's son, Rehoboam, became king. For a while, despite all the problems between north and south, the country remained united. But then, elders from the tribes north of Jerusalem had a meeting with King Rehoboam. They demanded that he reduce the heavy burden of taxes. Rehoboam refused. His attitude was proud and haughty.

This is the way Rehoboam responded to the demands that taxes be lowered. He said to the people:

> My father (meaning King Solomon) made your burden (of taxes) heavy; and I will add to that burden.
>
> My father punished you by striking you with whips; I will punish you with poisonous snakes.

This proud talk disturbed the northerners greatly. It stirred up a spirit of revolt. Jeroboam, who had been visiting Egypt, returned and became the leader of the revolt. The northern tribes knew that King Rehoboam was weak, and would not fight them, so they declared their independence, and made Jeroboam king over the 10 tribes in the northern portion of the country.

The people of Judah did not join the northerners. They remained loyal to King Rehoboam. He was, after all, the son of Solomon and grandson of David! He was their fellow tribesman and their friend.

The Judeans never changed their minds. As long as the kingdom lasted, a descendant of David reigned.

Thus, two Jewish nations came to live side by side. The one in the north was known as the Kingdom of Israel. The one in the south was called the Kingdom of Judah.

Judah was small in comparison to Israel. Its territory included the land of the tribe of Judah which was to the south of Jerusalem, and the land of the tribe of Benjamin, to the north of the city.

How Both Kingdoms Suffered

The division into two kingdoms was a terrible thing for both Israel and Judah. Both became weaker because of it.

The enemies of the Jews on the eastern side of the Jordan, whom David had conquered, renewed their attacks when they saw what had happened. The Arameans, especially those who lived close to the borders of Israel in the north, caused trouble for almost 200 years.

Judah, in the south, suffered a great deal too. Fortunately, its enemies, Moab, Edom and Egypt, were also plagued by troubles. Still, the Egyptians used every opportunity to attack Judah, and to destroy many of its cities. They also robbed the treasures of the Temple in Jerusalem.

Although Israel and Judah battled each other from time to time, there were occasions when they joined hands to fight against a common foe.

Having to fight often meant that it was necessary to maintain large armies, and to build new fortifications. This drained the energies of both kings, and was very expensive for both the Kingdom of Israel and the Kingdom of Judah. The people of both kingdoms had to pay high taxes and often had to work without pay because the government had no money.

Life in the Territory of Israel

In one way, the Jews of the Kingdom of Israel were better off than their fellow Jews in Judah. Some of the merchants in Israel had become great traders and they grew rich. The farmers of Israel had better soil than those in Judah, so more of them prospered. Nevertheless, the wealth of *some* Israelites became a curse. The rich became greedy, and stooped so low that they even robbed the poor.

Besides this, there were other problems in the territory of the Kingdom of Israel:

1. The enemies of Israel along their borders were powerful and ambitious. They constantly attacked the land and caused great damage.

2. The kings of Israel had no tradition to support their claims to the throne. Anyone who felt powerful enough to seek the throne did so. Many kings achieved their ambition to rule Israel by murdering the reigning king, and taking his place. Often, every member of the previous king's family was put to death! Kings who came to the throne in this way could not be loved. They were obeyed out of fear. They disgraced the name of Israel.

3. The Jewish religion in Israel reached a very low level. The kings of Israel were largely to blame. They did *not* want their people to go to the Temple in Jerusalem (which was in the territory of Judah) to worship God. They did *not* want their citizens to mix freely with the Jews of Judah who always visited the Temple.

Jeroboam, the very first king of Israel, built a place of worship—a sanctuary—in Beth El, about 10 miles northeast of Jerusalem. He chose this city because it was known as a holy place. The patriarch, Jacob, had once erected an altar to God there. Since the ark and the tablets on which the Ten Commandments were engraved were in the possession of the southern kingdom, King Jeroboam placed a golden bull in the sanctuary in Beth El.

Some Israelites believed the bull was an image of God and they worshipped it. But it was an idol, and many Jews got into the habit of worshiping idols. Before long, they stopped obeying God's commandments.

Life in the Territory of Judah

The Kingdom of Judah did not have the problems faced by the Kingdom of Israel.

1. Judah's enemies were generally weak, and Judah did not have to go to war against them very often.

2. The kings of Judah had to be descendants of King David, and so not very many outsiders tried to become king.

3. The religion of the people of Judah was strong because the Temple was in their territory—in Jerusalem. This was not enough to keep *all* the people faithful to God and the brit. Many *did* turn to idol worship. But, for the most part, the Judeans performed their religious duties more faithfully than the Israelites in the northern territory.

The Prophet—A New Kind of Jewish Leader

Few of the kings were great leaders. Had not the prophets appeared, Jewish history might have come to an end at this time as did the history of most of the nations that existed it those days.

About these prophets we shall learn more in our next unit.

These huge, reddish cliffs are one of the earliest sources of copper in the world, dating back to 4,500 B.C.E. The greatest period of copper production was during the reign of King Solomon, and because of this these mines are called King Solomon's Mines.

SUMMARY OF UNIT II

The Jews who settled in Eretz Yisrael 3,200 years ago were divided into independent tribes. However, all 12 tribes were friendly, and often helped one another.

The strongest bond between the tribes was their religion. They all worshipped God, and all felt it was their duty to obey the laws of the covenant.

The tribes had other things in common. They had a common language, common memories, and also common enemies.

When the Jews were attacked by the mighty Philistines, Samuel the Seer helped his people form a nation under a king. They thought that this would unite the tribes, bring victory over their enemies, and encourage the worship of God.

Saul, the first king, failed to help the Jews very much. The Philistines continued to oppress them. However, Saul's brief rule convinced the people that they must remain a united nation. They would be free only if they continued to be united.

So, after Saul, they chose another king; they chose David.

David accomplished great things. He defeated the enemy nations, and enlarged the land. He made Jews remember that God was their true ruler. To emphasize this, David brought the ark containing the Ten Commandment tablets to Jerusalem.

In addition, to prove to the people that God was the Ruler over all people, David honored the prophet Nathan. This was important because Nathan once scolded David for taking another man's wife. King David also stengthened the nation by improving its army and appointing many officials to help govern the land.

David became the most beloved ruler in the history of our people! Solomon became the king after David's death, and he kept peace in the land. He made Jerusalem a holy city by building a great and beautiful Temple there. But King Solomon overtaxed the people, and he made the tribes who lived in the northern part of Eretz Yisrael feel that they were less important than the southern tribes.

When Solomon died, the northern tribes formed the Kingdom of Israel, while the two tribes in the south, Judah and Benjamin, became the Kingdom of Judah. The nation had become divided. The division spelled trouble for both kingdoms.

A new kind of leader — a prophet — appeared. The words and deeds of the prophets were to change things for the Jewish people.

We shall learn about the prophets in our next unit.

2800 YEARS AGO SOLOMON
DIED. THE KINGDOM SPLIT
INTO ISRAEL AND JUDAH.

2800 YEARS AGO - PROPHET ELIJAH
TAUGHT THAT EVEN THE KING
MUST OBEY GOD AND BE JUST.

Introduction

WHAT THE PROPHETS SAID AND DID

Ever since the days of Abraham, almost 4,000 years ago, Jews remembered that they had a brit with God; and they relied on Him to protect them. Yet, only few knew and obeyed the mitzvot which God expected them to obey.

When Solomon built the glorious Temple in Jerusalem, many Jews made the mistake of thinking that God would make His home in the Temple. They felt sure that God would always protect it and the Jewish people. To influence God to remain in the Temple and protect His chosen people, the Jews brought sacrifices and celebrated festivals.

A very remarkable group of men, known as prophets, realized that God wanted the sacrifices of the people only when they were honest and kind. The prophets, therefore, demanded that Jews learn and obey all the

2700 YEARS AGO - AMOS, HOSEA AND ISAIAH PROPHESIED. ASSYRIA DESTROYED ISRAEL.

2600 YEARS AGO - AN ANCIENT SCROLL OF DEUTERONOMY WAS FOUND. SACRIFICE ALLOWED ONLY IN TEMPLE.

2550 YEARS AGO - JEREMIAH PROPHESIED, BABYLONIA CONQUERED AND EXILED JUDAH AND DESTROYED THE TEMPLE.

EZEKIEL COMFORTED THE EXILES. STUDY AND PRAYER REPLACED SACRIFICE AT THE TEMPLE.

mitzvot that were part of the brit with God. The prophets even threatened that God would destroy the Temple as well as the nation if the people failed to do what God asked of them.

2500 YEARS AGO - THE SECOND ISAIAH PROPHESIED. KING CYRUS ALLOWED THE JEWS TO RETURN TO JUDAH.

Just what did God want of His people? How did the prophets teach their people? How successful were they? Who were the great prophets? Unit Three will answer these questions.

THE TEMPLE WAS JOYOUSLY REBUILT. HAGGAI, ZECHARIAH AND MALACHI PROPHESIED.

89

This is the Gate of Mercy, located along the eastern wall of the Old City of Jerusalem. Some people believe the Prophet Elijah will enter Jerusalem through this gate when he returns as the Messiah.

CHAPTER 10

ELIJAH THE PROPHET BATTLES BAAL

Who Is a Prophet?

Back in 1897, the independent State of Israel did not yet exist. Jews dreamed about it, but did little to bring it into being. Theodor Herzl, about whom we shall learn later, held a meeting that year in Basel, Switzerland. About 200 Jews from all parts of the world attended. At that meeting, they agreed to try to establish a Jewish state. Herzl was so enthusiastic that he noted in his diary:

In Basel I established a Jewish state. If I were to say that aloud, universal laughter would be the response. Maybe in five years, certainly in fifty, everybody will recognize it.

Herzl was right. People did laugh at him when they first learned of his plan. Yet, 50 years later, in 1947, the United Nations *voted* to make a portion of ancient Eretz Yisrael a Jewish state. In 1948, Israel actually *became* an independent Jewish state!

Impressed by Herzl's remarkable foretelling of the future, some people called him a prophet. They were only *partly* right.

One characteristic of the prophets was their uncanny

ability to foresee events to come. Their most significant trait, however, was that they acted as God's spokesman. Speaking in God's name, they told the people what God wanted them to do.

And the prophets were not afraid. They spoke frankly to kings, noblemen, and all others who had to be reminded to obey God's mitzvot.

The Characteristics of a Prophet

What made the prophets so unusual was:

1. Their absolute faith in God. They believed He was merciful and just.
2. Their belief that they had to do whatever God asked, whether they liked it or not.
3. Their warnings that the brit with God would not protect them; that He would punish wicked Jews and destroy the Jewish kingdom if its inhabitants failed to act justly.
4. Their demand that *all* Jews, kings as well as ordinary persons, must keep the brit with God by obeying His mitzvot.
5. Their courage to defend the weak against the strong.
6. Their deep love for their fellow Jews and for Eretz Yisrael.
7. Their concern for the well-being of all mankind.

All of the prophets possessed many of these wonderful qualities.

The Early Prophets

There were many prophets whose words and deeds were never written down. Others, who lived more than

2,750 years ago, are mentioned only briefly in our Tanach.

The first great prophet was Moses. He lived 3,200 years ago and is honored as the greatest prophet who ever lived. He is also remembered as a great teacher and is, therefore, called Moshe Rabbenu—our teacher Moses.

The second of the great early prophets was Samuel the Seer. He lived about 3,000 years ago—200 years after Moses died.

Elijah: The Prophet Who Went to Heaven

Among the prophets whose speeches and acts are mentioned in the Tanach is Elijah. No doubt, you have heard of him. He is "expected" at every Pesach Seder. A special goblet, filled with wine, is set aside for him, and the door is opened to welcome him in.

The ceremony of welcoming Elijah during the Pesach Seder grew out of a strange legend. At the end of his life, our Tanach tells, Elijah went up to heaven in a fiery chariot! Because of this story, some ancient rabbis came to the conclusion that Elijah never died; that he continues to live in heaven, but occasionally visits the earth. He comes down when he learns that a righteous person is in trouble, or that a student needs help to learn more about God. He helps both.

Living in heaven, our ancestors believed, Elijah would be the first to know about the coming of the Messiah, and that Elijah will bring the good news to the Jewish people.

The fact that such stories were told about Elijah proves that Jews always loved him and respected him.

What did Elijah do to earn this great reputation?

The Kingdom of Israel in the Time of Ahab

Elijah lived in the Kingdom of Israel about 2,800 years ago. Israel was fairly strong then. It was at peace with Judah, but was at war with the Assyrians—a mighty nation.

Israel's king at this time was Ahab. Ahab had inherited the throne from his father who had overthrown the previous king. This kept happening among the kings of the Kingdom of Israel. One king killed another! Ahab was one of the few kings of Israel who neither murdered his predecessor, nor died by the hand of an assassin.

King Ahab lived in a beautiful palace, in the city of Samaria. His father had built it and fortified it. During the reign of Ahab, many merchants became rich and built comfortable homes. City people found jobs more readily than in the past. Farmers and keepers of orchards and vineyards prospered. Shepherds and herdsmen grazed their sheep and cattle in safety.

But a few individuals—men devoted to God—were unhappy. They were disturbed because large numbers of Jews were worshiping the idol called Baal. King Ahab knew about this, but was silent. He was supposed to keep the brit with God, and he knew that it was his responsibility to promote the worship of God. Yet, he even allowed a shrine to Baal to be built in Samaria. He did this in order to please his wife, Jezebel.

Jezebel was a Phoenician princess. Her marriage to Ahab was part of a peace treaty between Israel and the Phoenicians. Jezebel believed in the god, Baal, and she introduced Baal worship into the palace. Before long, it spread over the whole land. Jezebel succeeded so well that Baal replaced God in the hearts of many. She even persecuted Jews when they worshiped God. Many people, like Ahab, clung to God, but worshiped Baal as well.

Elijah Fights Baal Worship

Elijah was disturbed by what was happening. Dresssed in a hairy mantle, his hair and beard long, he suddenly appeared before King Ahab and warned him that God would punish him and his people for worshiping Baal.

"Let us find out who is the real God and who is not," said Elijah.

The king agreed, and at the king's command all people of Israel were told to assemble on Mount Carmel where the test was to take place. Our Tanach tells us what happened:

When the crowd was assembled, Elijah cried out: "How long will you people be undecided? Either worship God or worship Baal. You can't believe in both."

The people were silent.

Elijah then took an animal sacrifice and laid it on the wooden altar. But he did not start the fire.

"Now you do the same," he said to the believers in Baal. And they, too, prepared a sacrifice.

"I will call on the name of God," said Elijah, "and you call on the name of your god! Whoever is the true God will start a fire under his sacrifice. That will be proof that He is God."

From morning until evening, the believers of Baal cried out, "Oh, Baal, answer us!" But he did not answer. And no fire appeared on the altar.

Then Elijah called upon his God, and a fire came forth and burnt the offerings.

When Jezebel learned what happened, she threatened to kill Elijah. He fled to the desert. There, our Tanach relates, Elijah had a marvelous vision: A roaring windstorm suddenly arose. Elijah was unafraid. God, he knew, was not to be found in a storm. An earthquake followed. Elijah waited patiently. Then he became aware of a deep stillness, from which "a still small voice" reached him. Recognizing it as the voice of God, Elijah was reassured of God's nearness. His courage was renewed, and he returned to Samaria, the capital of the Kingdom of Israel.

Elijah's Defense of Justice

Shortly after his return, Elijah heard an ugly story. King Ahab had wanted to buy the vineyard of his neighbor, Naboth. But Naboth loved his property and refused to sell it. Jezebel, seeing the king's disappointment and believing that ordinary people counted for nothing, bribed some men to accuse Naboth of cursing God and the king. Naboth was found "guilty," and was put to death. Then, his property was taken over by the king.

Outraged by the injustice, Elijah hastened to the vineyard of the dead Naboth. He found King Ahab there, and he roared at him:

Thus says the Lord: "Have you murdered, and will you also take possession?"

He told the king that God will surely punish him for this evil deed. Ahab felt deeply ashamed.

Some time later, King Ahab was killed in a battle with one of Israel's foreign enemies—the Arameans.

Our Tanach tells much more about Elijah. Yet, we really know very little about him. Most of the stories in the Tanach are legends. There is no way of proving whether they actually happened. But this we do know about Elijah:

1. He had faith in God alone, and he had the courage to worship Him despite the threats of Queen Jezebel.
2. He went wherever he felt God wanted him to go, and he did what he believed God wanted him to do. He taught the people to worship God and not Baal.
3. He defended the weak against the strong, even against the king!

We Jews have good reason to remember and admire Elijah, and we do so every year at the Pesach seder.

Elijah was only partly successful. Some worshipers of Baal gave up idol worship, but many did not. In our next chapter, we shall learn that although Elijah worked hard at establishing justice in Israel, it did not take root. The people of Israel were heading for destruction.

CHAPTER 11

AMOS AND HOSEA:
PROPHETS WHO FOUGHT FOR JUSTICE

With Justice for All

The preamble to the Constitution of the United States tells us why, in 1776, the American colonies decided to break away from England and start a new government. The preamble says:

> We, the people of the United States, in order to form a more perfect Union, establish justice, insure domestic tranquility. . . .

To establish *justice* was one of the main reasons why our democratic form of government was created. The American colonies were not treated justly by the British. The British were not fair in many ways. For example, they wanted the people to pay taxes, but did not permit them to vote in elections.

Because people are not always treated justly, we have many problems even today. This is the reason why minority groups sometimes try to stir up a rebellion against the government in power.

In the Days of Kings and Prophets

The desire for justice is old. When the Jews confirmed

their brit with God on Mount Sinai, they agreed to act justly. That was part of accepting God and believing in Him.

We find, however, that kings ascended the throne of the Kingdom of Israel by murdering the former kings and their families.

In fact, shortly after King Ahab died in a battle against the Arameans, one of his officers killed Ahab's son, as well as Queen Jezebel and all the other members of Ahab's family. The officer was eager to win the support of the prophets, so he also had all worshipers of Baal put to death! This awful massacre sent a shudder through all the citizens of Israel, including the very people it was intended to please—the worshipers of God. This unjust act made Israel weaker.

Somehow, this assassin-king managed to hold the throne for almost 30 years. His son followed him as king and his grandson also. Thirty years later, his great-grandson, Jeroboam II, became King of Israel and reigned for 40 years. Jeroboam II is remembered for three reasons:

1. During his reign, there was peace in the land. This happened because Israel's enemies, the Assyrians, had crippled another of Israel's enemies, the Arameans. Then, the Assyrians became involved in other wars. This enabled Jeroboam II to improve conditions in his own land.

2. He maintained friendly relations with the Kingdom of Judah.

3. Caravans once again traveled the highways of Israel in peace, and they brought wealth to the

land. Trade increased, and the rich grew richer.

The powerful and the rich praised Jeroboam II. But the poor and the weak: the worker, the farmer, and the shepherd, who were the majority of Israel, suffered greatly.

Unexpectedly, a mighty voice cried out in their behalf. The voice came from the sanctuary in Beth El and was heard throughout the land.

The Prophet Amos Demands Justice

It happened a few years before Jeroboam II died, when Israel was enjoying peace and prosperity. A huge crowd of happy people, dressed in their finest, was gathered before the sanctuary to bring offerings to God. Suddenly, the crowd was startled by the loud, strong voice as it proclaimed:

This is the word of God! The Arameans, the Moabites, and the Edomites have acted cruelly and unjustly to one· another and to their neighbors. God will, therefore, destroy them all!

These were old enemies of Israel that the prophet was talking about. The pronouncement of their doom pleased the people assembled at Beth El. But the voice continued:

The same fate awaits Judah!

This shook the people! It was totally unexpected. The Kingdom of Israel was at peace with the Kingdom of Judah. Some Israelites even made pilgrimages to Jerusalem in Judah to worship God in His holy Temple! And then came the final note of doom as Amos cried out:

The Kingdom of Israel will soon fall!

The people at Beth El were stunned. Can this man,

Amos, who *sounds* like a prophet, be a *true* prophet? Was God *really* speaking through him?

The people wondered: How can we be destroyed? Do we not have a brit with almighty God assuring us of His protection as long as we worship Him? And we are surely worshiping Him! We celebrate the festivals and we bring Him sacrifices.

The speaker answered their unspoken questions.

I, Amos, am not a professional prophet who expects to be paid. I earn my livelihood by selling wool, by caring for trees, and by herding cattle in my hometown in Judah. I speak only at God's command, and say only what He tells me. You are wrong in believing that you are worshiping God when you disregard His mitzvot. You are not acting justly, and you refuse to treat the poor and the weak with kindness. Your failure to obey God's mitzvot cannot be forgiven merely because you bring him sacrifices. Sacrifices are acceptable only *after* you stop doing things that hurt your fellow men.

Without mincing words, Amos told them in detail the wrong things that they were doing:

1. Your merchants cheat both their suppliers and their customers.
2. You lend money at high interest. When the poor cannot repay, you take away their land, or whatever they own, and make them your servants.
3. The rich people among you live in luxury, while the poor lack bread.
4. You act unjustly. You bribe the judges to favor you, and then you bring sacrifices to God to remove His anger from you.

Amos warned the people that God could not be bribed like crooked judges. He told them that He would not accept their sacrifices, because they were unfaithful to the brit. He also warned them that since they promised to obey God's commandments, and failed to do so, God would punish them more severely than those who never entered into the brit.

Israel will fall, Amos warned, unless Jews stop doing evil, and begin doing good.

For the most part, Amos' message fell on deaf ears. The chief priest at Beth El accused Amos of treason, and drove him out of Israel. But there were Jews who knew Amos was speaking the truth. They were convinced that God had instructed him to say the things he was saying.

The words of Amos were written down, and are included in our Tanach. They continue to impress us to this day.

Quarreling Groups in Israel

A few years after Amos pronounced the downfall of Israel, King Jeroboam II died. His son followed him as king and was murdered. The king that followed Jeroboam's son was also murdered.

The Kingdom of Israel was torn into quarreling groups, each seeking power. Injustices and cruelty were widespread. The brit with God was neglected. The worship of Baal grew more popular.

The strife in Israel could not have happened at a worse time. Israel's old and mighty enemy, Assyria, suddenly grew in power. It crushed its neighbors to the north, south and east, and prepared to march west, to the lands of the Arameans, the Israelites, and the Judeans.

The Prophet Hosea Pleads in Vain

In the midst of this turmoil, the Prophet Hosea tried to restore peace in Israel by uniting all Jews in the worship of God alone. Like Amos, Hosea declared that God had told him what to say. He spoke gently and honestly. God loves the Jews, Hosea assured his listeners. That is why He entered into a brit with us. We are like a beautiful bride in His eyes. And then he stormed:

> But we have not behaved properly. We were unfaithful to Him and worshiped Baal. We paid no attention to God's wishes and acted unjustly.

Gently, Hosea went on:

> Let us resolve to return to the worship of God.
> Let us not try to bribe Him with sacrifices.
> Let us obey His mitzvot.
> Let us again become His beloved people.

When Hosea observed that the injustices, the strife, and the worship of Baal continued, he thundered:

Israel is doomed.

It will soon be destroyed.

The Kingdom of Israel Is Destroyed

Amos and Hosea were soon proved right. After 200 years as a nation, Israel was conquered by Assyria. Its cities were destroyed, and tens of thousands of the Israelites were taken captive to far-off Assyria. The Kingdom of Israel disappeared from the earth. Its people, commonly known as the Ten Lost Tribes of Israel, were never heard of again.

These descendants of the Samaritans live in Nablus (called Shechem in Bible times). Above, they are celebrating the holiday of Shavuot.

The Samaritans

What really happened to all those Jews?

They didn't *actually* disappear! Most of the captives remained in the former Kingdom of Israel and were mixed with other captives whom the Assyrians brought in from other lands. Those Jews who stayed on in Israel became known as Samaritans. They were called by that name because Samaria was the capital of Israel.

To this day a small number of Samaritans still live in Israel, in the city called Nablus. In the Bible, Nablus is called Shechem.

The religion of the Samaritans is similar to Judaism in some ways, but is different in other ways. Only the Five Books of Moses and the Book of Joshua are part of *their* Bible. They also worship God somewhat differently from Jews. To this day, on Pesach, they celebrate the deliverance from Egypt by actually sacrificing and eating sheep, as Jews did in Bible days.

The history of the ancient Kingdom of Israel is now at an end. Jews, however, survived the catastrophe. The Jewish religion, and its ways of life, continued on in Judah. And so, it is to Judah that we now turn for a continuation of the story of our people.

CHAPTER 12

ISAIAH: A PROPHET WHO
WAS ALWAYS HOPEFUL

Alongside the United Nations buildings in New York, there is an inscription that reads:

> THEY SHALL BEAT THEIR SWORDS INTO PLOWSHARES AND THEIR SPEARS INTO PRUNING HOOKS. NATION SHALL NOT LIFT UP SWORD AGAINST NATION, NEITHER SHALL THEY LEARN WAR ANY MORE.

The hope for world peace that is expressed in this inscription was first spoken by two prophets who lived in the Kingdom of Judah: Isaiah and Micah.

Will God Always Protect His People?

We do not know which of these two prophets was the first to utter these words, and it is really not important. What *is* important is that both Isaiah and Micah were great prophets, and both were very anxious to see peace come to the world. Both were heartbroken as they watched the Kingdom of Israel being destroyed by greedy Assyria.

Along with other Judeans in the south, they were filled with fear. They wondered why God let this misfortune happen to Israel—to their fellow Jews who lived in the north. According to the brit, God was expected to *protect* the Jews.

And then, the people started asking the terrifying question: Will God no longer protect the people of the covenant? Will God no longer protect the Jewish people? Might not the people of Judah suffer the same fate as their brothers of the north?

Isaiah answered their questions. But he was a stern prophet, and did not offer too much comfort to his people. God, Isaiah said to the Judeans, did not stop protecting the Kingdom of Israel. Israel was destroyed because its people had failed to live according to God's mitzvot. They brought about their own downfall!

Most Judeans who heard Isaiah felt better. God had not deserted them, and He would not desert them in the future. He could be relied upon to protect them as long as they were loyal to the brit.

Still, many Jews were worried. If Isaiah is right, they thought, God will not protect Jews simply because they are His people. He will protect them only if they obey the mitzvot of the brit. And if this is true, these Judeans wondered, why will Judah be spared? Are the people of Judah any better that those of Israel?

In many ways, the people of the Kingdom of Judah thought they *were* better than their fellow Jews who had lived in the Kingdom of Israel.

Why Judeans Thought They Were Safe

Ever since the days of David, the kings of Judah had been worshipers of God, even though there were times when they also worshiped Baal. Often the kings permitted the Judeans to do so.

The kings of Judah, unlike those of Israel, never ascended the throne by murdering the reigning ruler. All kings of Judah were sons of kings who reigned before them.

Judeans always remembered the special brit God had made with David, in which He promised that only David's descendants would rule the country. They were glad to see the promise fulfilled, and never wanted to place anyone on the throne who was not of David's family.

The people in Judah also felt secure because they were not involved in as many wars as the Jewish kingdom of the north.

Finally, the people in Judah were not divided into rich and poor classes as were the people of Israel. Few of Judah's citizens were *very* wealthy, and few were *very* poor.

The Prophets Despair

Perhaps Judah *was* better than Israel, but still Isaiah and Micah found much that was wrong. The people of Judah had not been faithful to the brit with God.

Isaiah was angry at them when he saw that the Judeans believed that God would be pleased with them if they prayed and brought sacrifices when, at the same time, they were mistreating their fellowman. He accused them of being cruel to the poor, of taking away other men's fields, of judging unfairly, and of worshiping other gods. Isaiah warned the worshipers that God would reject their prayers if they acted wickedly.

Micah spoke out very strongly too. Like Isaiah and the prophets before him, Micah scolded the rich for oppressing the poor and even robbing them of the little they had. He lashed out at people who spoke lies.

Both Isaiah and Micah prophesied that, because of the evil in the land, Judah would fall as did Israel. God cannot tolerate evil!

Isaiah did say, however, that Judah possessed some virtues. He said that a number of Judeans were faithful to the brit and did observe the mitzvot. Therefore, he concluded, the destruction of Judah would not be *total*. A remnant of Judah would survive.

To be sure that this would happen, Isaiah advised:
Cease to do evil;
Learn to do good.
Seek justice;
Relieve the oppressed.
Micah agreed and urged:
Do justly;
Love mercy;
And walk humbly with your God.

The Assyrian Invasion

Twenty years after the fall of Israel, Assyria invaded Judah. Hezekiah was king of Judah at the time. Like his father, and like other kings of the region, Hezekiah had been paying taxes to Assyria to keep it from invading Judah.

But Hezekiah grew tired of pouring out so much money from the treasury each year. Relying on help from Egypt, Hezekiah rebelled against the King of Assyria. Thereupon, a huge Assyrian army descended upon Judah.

Isaiah watched King Hezekiah's preparations for revolt with a sinking heart. He feared that Assyria would destroy Judah and exile its people. Desperately, he urged the king to give up his plans to revolt. Isaiah told the king that it is better to rely on God than on men and horses; that Egypt will not help the people of Israel.

When Hezekiah insisted on going ahead with his plan, Isaiah dressed up like a captive and walked the streets. It was his way of protesting against the king's actions. When people stopped and stared, Isaiah warned them that if Judah rebelled against Assyria, all the citizens of Israel would end up as captives.

Assyria Cannot Capture Jerusalem

Judah did rebel, and the Assyrians came. Their armies quickly captured and destroyed dozens of Judean cities, and soon surrounded Jerusalem. The Assyrian official who was sent by his king demanded the surrender of the city. He shouted up to the defenders on the walls: "You are few in number, you have little equipment. You lack even food and water."

His information was correct, except about the water. King Hezekiah had dug a long tunnel through solid rock, and brought fresh spring water into Jerusalem from the other side of the walls. This tunnel was rediscovered almost a hundred years ago, and is called the Pool of Siloam.

Hearing no response from the Judeans, the Assyrian commander continued: "What makes you Judeans believe you can resist my mighty army? Do you rely on your god? You are fools if you do. The gods of other nations could not stop us! Yours won't either!"

The Tanach tells us that Isaiah was enraged at the Assyrian's insult to God. He assured Hezekiah that God would protect Jerusalem, because the Assyrians had mocked Him. Jerusalem did *not* fall.

The Assyrian army withdrew. One reason given is that a plague swept through the army and the Assyrian soldiers were too sick to fight. Another reason is that the Assyrian king had to move his army to defend himself against other subjects who had revolted elsewhere. At any rate, Jerusalem was saved and the Kingdom of Judah was spared—for a while.

The people of Judah rejoiced. God had delivered them from the mighty Assyrians. They were now confident that God would continue to protect His people.

But, Isaiah remained gloomy. The Jews were still not living up to the demands of the covenant. He was sure that they were not likely to change, and that disaster would soon come upon them.

The Prophet's Hope

There were, however, righteous Jews in Judah. For this small group, for this remnant, Isaiah saw hope. This hope was shared by Micah: "The remnant will never disappear. God will spare them and they will continue to

This section from the Book of Isaiah is part of the Dead Sea Scrolls, which were discovered in 1947. The section dates back to between 100 B.C.E. and 100 C.E.

obey His mitzvot. Peace and the good life will then come to the world."

Both Isaiah and Micah expressed the same idea in these words:

They shall beat their swords into plowshares,
And their spears into pruning hooks.

Major and Minor Prophets

Isaiah's prophecies and acts are all recorded in a large volume consisting of many chapters. For this reason, Isaiah is now called a "major" prophet. Micah's speeches make up a small book, and he was called a "minor" prophet. Both, however were great men and great prophets.

What finally happened to our people after they learned from Isaiah and Micah that the brit would be respected by God only if Judah was governed by His mitzvot? Our next chapter will tell us what happened. We will learn of the part played by another great prophet, Jeremiah, whom we respect to this day for his forthrightness, for his love of God, and for his concern for the Jewish People.

CHAPTER 13

JEREMIAH: THE PROPHET WHO LIVED IN THE WORST OF TIMES

A Day of Fasting

Tisha B'Av—the ninth day of the Jewish month of Av—is a day of fasting in the Jewish calendar. It usually falls during the hot days of late July or early August. Lights in many synagogues are dimmed. In others, people sit on the floor or on overturned benches. They all listen to the sad words being read from the Book of Lamentations.

This book of the Bible expresses the horror and pain caused by the destruction of the Kingdom of Judah. We do not know who wrote the Book of Lamentations, although many people think its author was the Prophet Jeremiah. Jeremiah lived through those terrible years.

Assyria Threatens Judea

Isaiah predicted the destruction of Judah 150 years before it happened. He was convinced that Assyria would destroy Judah — just as it had destroyed the Kingdom of Israel — but he was wrong. Judah was destroyed, but *not* by Assyria.

Assyria did attack Judah and its capital city, Jerusalem,

but Judah survived that attack. King Hezekiah's son prevented another Assyrian invasion years later by paying a tax to Assyria, and by permitting the worship of Assyrian gods in Judah.

Pious Jews were disturbed over this, but could do little to change the situation. Little by little, more and more Judeans worshiped idols and performed evil deeds. These actions were condemned by Isaiah and Micah.

Discovery of Deuteronomy

About fifty years after Hezekiah's death, things suddenly changed. A dramatic discovery was made! While the Temple in Jerusalem was being repaired, an old scroll was found. It was brought to Josiah who was the king at that time. We now believe that the scroll was part of the Book of Deuteronomy, one of the Five Books of Moses. It was a holy book, and its contents terrified the king.

What frightened King Josiah more than anything else was the demand that God alone was to be worshiped, and that all offerings be made only to Him in the Temple in Jerusalem. The Book of Deuteronomy warned that all who did not obey this commandment would be severely punished, and the kingdom itself would be destroyed!

King Josiah took drastic action. He immediately outlawed all idol worship and ordered that all places of worship outside of the Temple be torn down. Josiah's orders were strictly enforced, and most of the idol worship came to an end.

Those who believed in God were highly pleased with King Josiah. The Prophet Jeremiah, who lived at that time, was also happy—but only for a short time. He lost his enthusiasm when he noticed that:

1. People who lived at a distance from the Temple, especially those living outside of Jerusalem, found it difficult to come to the Temple. Since they knew of no other way to worship God, many stopped worshiping Him altogether.

2. The priests did not teach those people who could not come to the Temple to obey the truly important mitzvot: to be just, kind, and truthful.

3. People felt certain that God would always protect the Temple since it was the only place of worship in the land. They also felt that God would protect Jerusalem and Judah as well.

4. People were overconfident that neither the Temple nor their land would ever fall into enemy hands.

Jeremiah knew better. Worship of God in the Temple was good only *if* it taught the worshipers to obey all of God's mitzvot. But, like many prophets before him, he saw that Jews who came to the Temple cheated and lied. He saw them oppress the defenseless. Even priests who led their fellow Jews in worship often did evil things. They misled the people by assuring them that God would forgive their sins if they brought sacrifices! And Jeremiah knew why. The priests received a portion of every offering, and they were greedy for more.

Jeremiah's Threat

Jeremiah hesitated before speaking out. He knew that few would listen. He knew, too, that he would be hated for what he had to say. He was prepared for that, too. He realized that his words would hurt his fellow Jews whom he loved dearly.

However, Jeremiah heard God command him to speak out. God's message burned within him like a blazing flame. He had to speak out. With a heavy heart,

Jeremiah made his way to the Temple. He saw large crowds bringing offerings, and speaking with confidence about their future. They felt the Temple was their guarantee of safety.

Jeremiah spoke:

Thus says God: Improve your conduct! Do not trust the liars who say: 'The Temple is God's; He will not let it be harmed; We are safe!' Can you be foolish enough to believe that God will accept the prayers of thieves, murderers, liars and idol-worshipers?

Jeremiah continued to speak:

Unless you obey God's mitzvot by living

righteously, Judah will fall into the hands of an enemy, and the Temple will not protect you. It will be destroyed just as the sanctuary in Shiloh was destroyed in the time of Samuel the Seer.

Jeremiah's words struck like thunder. His listeners were furious and wanted to lynch him. Voices denounced Jeremiah as a traitor. Many wanted him put to death. Unexpectedly, the king's officers saved Jeremiah, and called for a public trial.

Jeremiah protested that he loved his God and his people. He had foretold the destruction because God had ordered him to do so.

Then, one old man spoke up: "Long ago," he said, "there lived a prophet named Micah. He had predicted the fall of Judah, yet no harm had come to Micah. Jeremiah, too, should be freed."

The court respected the old man, and agreed with him. They set Jeremiah free.

Jeremiah Continues to Prophesy

The prophet continued speaking but he was not believed. He then had his scribe record the prophetic words and read them aloud. Officers of the king seized the document, but allowed Jeremiah's scribe to depart in peace. Jeremiah's words were then read to the king. Enraged, he cut Jeremiah's message to pieces and burned it.

Jeremiah dictated his words again, and added a threat:

The Babylonians, who had recently risen to great power and had overthrown the once mighty Assyria, would become God's instrument for destroying Judah and its Temple.

Although, in his days, neither the king nor the people believed him, Jeremiah is a "major" prophet. His words are part of one of the large books of the Bible.

Before long, the Babylonians invaded Judah and carried off the king together with thousands of officials and skilled workers. One of the captives brought to Babylonia was a prophet named Ezekiel. We shall learn more about him in our next chapter.

Zedekiah was appointed by the Babylonians to replace the captive king and to sit on the throne of Judah. It was clearly understood that Judah was to pay an annual tribute to the treasury of the king of Babylonia.

Zedekiah Plans to Revolt

King Zedekiah was not satisfied with being a Babylonian puppet-king. He plotted a revolt. Word of Zedekiah's intentions reached the Jews in Babylonia. Many of them began to hope for an early return to their beloved Judah.

Jeremiah crushed their hopes. He sent the Jews of Babylonia a letter saying:

Be patient! Settle yourselves down in Babylonia. Promote the welfare of the country. Only in this way will you enjoy peace. The return to Judah is many years away.

King Zedekiah persisted in his plans. Jeremiah talked against the king, and the king threw him into a dungeon. Jeremiah was certain that the land of Judah would be destroyed and the people exiled. Nevertheless, he believed that one day in the future Jews would reoccupy Eretz Yisrael. To prove that he really believed what he preached, Jeremiah purchased a piece of land—in Eretz Yisrael—even while he was a prisoner!

When King Zedekiah released Jeremiah from prison, the prophet put a harness on his own neck. Those who saw Jeremiah and the yoke on his neck cried out:

We agree! We must bear the yoke of Babylonian rule!

If we revolt, it will only bring destruction to our land.

Zedekiah did not agree. He refused to pay tribute to the Babylonians, and an army was sent in to capture Jerusalem. Jeremiah then prophesied that the city would fall and be destroyed.

Jeremiah sounded like a traitor. Zedekiah, at the urging of his officers, placed Jeremiah in a deep, muddy pit. They expected him to die. But a servant of the king saved the prophet. After a while, with the approval of Zedekiah, Jeremiah was set free.

The Great Babylonian Captivity

In the year 586 B.C.E. (that is, 586 years before the year 1—the year of the Common Era), over 2,550 years ago, on the ninth day of Av (now observed as Tisha

B'Av), the Babylonians broke through the walls of Jerusalem, killed thousands of its inhabitants, and burnt the Temple. Soon after, they captured and blinded King Zedekiah, and brought him to Babylonia along with thousands of other Judean captives.

This was the way the Babylonian captivity, which lasted 50 years, began. The Babylonians allowed only the weak and the poor, who would never be able to revolt again, to remain in Judah. Jeremiah stayed on with this group in Judah, or in *Judea*, as Judah was often called.

Judah's troubles were not yet ended. The Babylonians

appointed a Jewish governor over the small Jewish community that remained in the vicinity of Jerusalem. Before long, he was murdered. Fearing punishment, most of the remaining Jews in Judea fled to Egypt. They forced Jeremiah to go along with them.

The once rich land of Judah was left in ruins. The

destruction was complete. The prophets had warned the kings and the people that this would happen—and it did happen.

Jeremiah—a True Prophet

As we review the life of Jeremiah, we cannot help but wonder: Why did he call the Jews murderers, thieves, liars and idol-worshipers? Surely he knew that most Jews were innocent of such crimes. Why did he continue to accuse them of injustice and cruelty? Many of his own personal experiences proved the opposite!

The king's officers saved him from the angry crowd when he predicted the destruction of the Temple. They had even judged him fairly and set him free. And again, when he was in the muddy pit, King Zedekiah was kind enough to save his life. There *was* justice in the land. Many acts of kindness were performed.

Jeremiah *knew* that Jews were not more wicked than other peoples. He also knew that most of them worshipped God. He was sure that many of those who brought offerings to other gods really thought they were worshiping God. But, as a prophet and as a leader, he was not satisfied. To him, the Jews were not as faithful, as kind, or as fair, as they *should* be, or could become, if they tried hard enough.

There is another strange side to Jeremiah, the prophet. He had never *wanted* to call his people wicked, or to forecast the destruction of the land and Temple. Why then did he do so?

The answer is given by Jeremiah himself: "God had so commanded me." Loving his fellow Jews, Jeremiah often prayed, asking God to be more merciful. Occasionally, the prophet even argued with God, as did Abraham, Moses and others. His prayers and arguments did not help. God, Jeremiah sadly realized, had to punish the Jewish people for their many faults.

But Jeremiah learned something from all this. He discovered that God did not want to bring calamity upon His people! He did so only to force them to try harder to improve their conduct — to *be* good and to *do* good.

Jeremiah was a wise and wonderful man, as well as a great prophet. It is too bad that most people did not appreciate him during his lifetime — 2,550 years ago.

CHAPTER 14
RETURNING TO THE LAND

On November 2, 1917, the Jews of the world were happy and excited. Lord Balfour, a high British official, had sent a brief note to the president of the English Zionist Federation. The president was an English scientist named Chaim Weizmann. The note promised that Great Britain would help the Jews build a homeland in Palestine. (Palestine was the name given to Eretz Yisrael by the conquering Romans.)

The Proclamation of Cyrus

The Balfour Declaration was not the first time such a promise was made to Jews. In 538 B.C.E., a little over 2,500 years ago, Cyrus, the Persian king who conquered Babylonia, issued a proclamation which is recorded in our Tanach. It stated:

> Whosoever there is among you all God's people ... let him go up to Jerusalem, which is in Judah, and build the house of the Lord ...

Cyrus not only encouraged Jews living in Babylonia to return to Judah (or Judea as the territory was often called), but promised to *help* those who wanted to go. In addition, he proved his sincerity by returning thousands of gold and silver vessels taken from the Temple by the Babylonians.

The offer was accepted. Thousands upon thousands of Jews faced the hardships of travel and made the *aliyah* (the ascent to Eretz Yisrael). They were going home! This was the first time people who had been *exiled* from its homeland had ever returned!

The Four Aliyot

Almost four thousand years ago, Abraham and his tribe made the first aliyah. The second aliyah, you remember, was made centuries later (about 3,200 years ago) under the leadership of Moses and Joshua.

The aliyah initiated by King Cyrus of Persia was the third in the series of *aliyot*. (Aliyot is the plural form of aliyah.) At the present time, the Jews returning to Israel represent the fourth aliyah. From every corner of the globe, including America, Jews are going to Israel. The attachment to Eretz Yisrael is very old and very strong.

Jewish Life in Babylonia

Babylonian Jews of the third aliyah—2,500 years ago— were anxious to return because they loved Eretz Yisrael. They wanted to return to the only place where they could worship God as free people, *and* in their own Temple!

Jews had arrived in Babylonia as prisoners of war about 50 years earlier. After walking a thousand miles from their homeland, they were weary to the bone, and they were fearful of what the future might have in store for them.

To the great surprise of the exiled Jews, their Babylonian captors had not put them in chains. Only a few were imprisoned. All others were given homes in towns and villages. They were allowed to work and earn their bread. They were even permitted to form Jewish communities and to continue to worship their own God.

After a while, Jews were no longer in fear of the Babylonians. In fact, they began to respect their captors, and they loved the fertile land. When they entered the cities of Babylonia they were impressed by the smooth, stone-covered streets. The beautiful buildings and glorious temples were greatly admired by the Judean prisoners of war. Even their beloved Jerusalem, with its great Temple, seemed insignificant in comparison. Babylonia was more wonderful than any place the Jews had ever imagined.

Feeling At Home in Babylonia

As the years passed, the memories of their sufferings at the hands of the Babylonian soldiers gradually faded, and the prosperity and feelings of security in Babylonia increased. Without realizing it, their love for their homeland, and devotion to their brit with God was getting weaker.

Although some of the Jews who lived in Babylonia did forget Jerusalem and their brit with God, the large majority did not! Most found the idol worship of the Babylonians to be utter nonsense. They were sure that it was far better to worship God.

Some Jews considered the idea of building a Temple in Babylonia, but this was ruled out. The Book of

Deuteronomy did not permit the erection of a Temple anywhere but in Jerusalem.

Without a Temple to go to, how could the Jews of Babylonia worship God? Two prophets arose among the Jews in Babylonia. They helped find the answer.

The Prophet Ezekiel

The first prophet in Babylonia was Ezekiel. He was brought to Babylonia as a captive. He was greatly respected, and Jews visited him, occasionally, especially on Shabbat. They came to hear him speak, or to listen to him read from holy books. Some of these readings were probably from the Book of Deuteronomy, from the earlier prophets, from the psalms, or from other scrolls. The words he read told of God, His concern for mankind, and His brit with His chosen people.

These meetings with Ezekiel encouraged and inspired the Jews of Babylonia. The word spread, and other meetings were arranged. If Ezekiel could not come to a meeting, others led in the readings and spoke words of praise to God. They thanked God for favoring them with the brit, and for His good teachings. At other times, they thanked God for their good fortune and begged His forgiveness for any bad actions.

The Beginnings of the Synagogue

In the course of years, the Babylonian exiles learned to meet often for study and prayer. They could not use either the Siddur or the Tanach to guide them at their religious assemblies. These books did not exist yet. However, their meetings on Sabbaths and holidays, when no Jew worked, became frequent. And so, perhaps without realizing what he had done, Ezekiel guided our

Babylonian ancestors into laying the foundations of the synagogue.

Ezekiel's Valley of Dry Bones

Ezekiel taught the Babylonian Jews to worship God. But, he also insisted that they worship God in holiness. Jews would have to return to Eretz Yisrael, he believed, and they would have to rebuild the Temple in Jerusalem.

Many Jews were sad and depressed. The Jewish nation was practically dead! How could they ever return to Eretz Yisrael?

Ezekiel comforted them by telling them about a glorious vision which he saw. He found himself, one day, in a mysterious valley littered with dry bones. At the command of God, the bones drew together, took on flesh, and stood up! They became living, breathing, human beings!

Ezekiel explained:

> The Jewish nation is like the dry bones. Its people is widely scattered. Like the dry bones, however, God will cause His people to reassemble and rise again as a Jewish nation!

Thus encouraged, the Babylonian Jews remained faithful to the brit. They were now hopeful that one day they would return to Eretz Yisrael.

The Second Isaiah

Then came an electrifying prophecy from the mouth of a second prophet whose *name* was lost, but whose *words* are recorded in chapters 40-66 of the Book of Isaiah. He became known as the Second Isaiah. The words of the First Isaiah are recorded in chapters 1-39.

We Jews, said the Second Isaiah, are not as good as we should be. God, however, feels that we have suffered enough. We have received enough punishment.

To prove that God still loves His chosen people, said the Second Isaiah, He will re-establish them in their own land. When they are resettled in Eretz Yisrael, they will then prove to the world that God is the only real God of the world, and that He created the universe.

The Second Isaiah then predicted that Cyrus, the ruler of Persia, would conquer the Babylonian empire. He would soon, thereafter, permit the Jews to return to Eretz Yisrael.

Isaiah's prophecy proved to be exactly right!

After the announcement was made that the Jews of Babylonia would be allowed to return to Eretz Yisrael, the question arose: How many would be willing to accept King Cyrus' invitation? After living there for 50 years, the Babylonian Jews felt quite comfortable. They were at home there!

The Third Return

For many of the Jews of Babylonia, the decision was simple. By the tens of thousands, the Jews of Babylonia sold their possessions. Hastily, they packed their belongings on donkeys and on camels, and joined the long trek back to Eretz Yisrael, the land they loved. They were marching back to Jerusalem so that they might worship God once again in His holy Temple. They were going home!

The majority of Babylonian Jews, however, stayed behind. They were too comfortable, and they did not want to give up their comforts. But, they gave support to the aliyah with generous gifts.

Can you imagine how those who were returning felt? The poet wrote about it in the Bible, in the Book of Psalms. He said:

> We were like dreamers . . .
> Our mouths were filled with laughter,
> Songs rolled off our tongues!

With hopes high, the Jews of the third aliyah returned to Eretz Yisrael. When they finally arrived, they were surprised at what they found.

CHAPTER 15

GREAT DREAMS AND REAL LIFE

Big Dreamers and Great Dreams

President Woodrow Wilson once said:

We grow great by dreams . . .

Some of us let great dreams die, but others
nourish and protect them . . .

Big men may be dreamers; not all dreamers are
big men.

We must judge the dreamer by his ability to stick
with his dream until it becomes a reality.

Those Jews who dreamed of re-establishing the Jewish
nation in Eretz Yisrael 2,500 years ago were certainly big
dreamers. But were they big enough to keep their dreams
alive?

On their way back to Eretz Yisrael, the Jews of
Babylonia talked a great deal about their great dreams:

1. They would rebuild the Temple.
2. They would beautify Jerusalem.
3. They would make Eretz Yisrael strong and
   prosperous.
4. They would re-establish a nation under the rule
   of a descendant of David.

The Harsh Realities of Life

Their glorious dreams were all but shattered by the harsh realities that the returning Jews had to face. They were shocked by what they saw.

1. The Temple, burned down years earlier, was still in ruins on Mount Zion—the holy mountain.
2. Comfortable homes and beautiful palaces that had not been completely demolished were now charred heaps of rubble.
3. The market places were all but empty.

Although the returnees found their homeland in ruins, they still held fast to their dream. After all, they *were* back in their homeland! There *were* standing on Mount Zion, the holiest spot in the whole world.

With prayers of thanksgiving and joyous song, they set out in search of their homes. But so many of them were disappointed!

1. Many homes had been taken over by Jews who had stayed on in Eretz Yisrael, and had not been forced to go into exile.
2. Some returning Jews found that their land was taken over by non-Jews who had drifted into Eretz Yisrael from neighboring countries.
3. Most returnees found their old homes, but could not prove ownership. While searching for proof, they had to live in shacks. Those who could not find proof had to build new homes.
4. Those who could prove ownership made enemies of those who were forced to leave their houses and farms.
5. Some returnees found their homes empty and badly in need of costly repairs. Getting settled proved to be very difficult.

The Building of a New Temple

Yet, when the autumn holidays came, Jews forgot their troubles for a while. They assembled on Mount Zion for the Sukkot holiday. They erected an altar upon which priests offered sacrifices to God. They were once again able to worship God on Mount Zion!

The returnees were now ready for the big project that had fired their imagination when they were still in Babylonia: The building of a new and beautiful Temple. They wanted it to be as beautiful as the First Temple built by King Solomon.

Workmen were engaged. The necessary materials were purchased. Soon the foundations of the Temple were laid. But again, many problems developed:

1. Much of the building material, promised by King Cyrus of Persia, had not arrived.
2. The Samaritans—the people living in the former Kingdom of Israel, and who were a mixture of Jews and non-Jews — offered to help build the Temple. The Jews refused their offer, because they wanted only true Jews to have a share in rebuilding the Temple. Feeling insulted, the Samaritans tried to stop the work. They even sent a message to the Persian king, but he did not pay attention to the Samaritans.
3. Non-Jewish people, who had taken over much of the land of Judah, made frequent raids on Jewish homes, causing much damage and heavy losses.
4. Crops did not grow well, and the people suffered from hunger and poverty.
5. The poor could not pay their taxes or repay loans. Many lost their property and were forced to become slaves.
6. Many wealthy people became even richer at the expense of the poor. They built themselves fine houses, bought up fields at cheap prices, and surrounded themselves with servants.

All these problems led to the neglect of the Temple. Yet, hope remained! From time to time new groups of Jews came to Judea from Babylonia and they brought with them hope and enthusiasm.

The Prophets Speak Out

Then, the prophet Haggai raised his voice in the name of God. "The Temple must be built at once," he cried.

Haggai warned that God is displeased with the rich who live in fine houses, while the Temple is left unfinished.

Haggai was joined by the prophet Zechariah. God will dwell in our midst and make us into a great nation, Zechariah said, if the Jews will undertake the rebuilding of the Temple.

The Jews listened to these prophets. The dream of a second Temple sprang to life. Everyone was filled with new hope, and worked hard at the task of rebuilding the Temple. And, finally—70 years after its destruction—the Temple was rebuilt.

A model of the Second Temple which was rebuilt during the life of King Herod. The model can be seen on the grounds of the Holyland Hotel in Jerusalem.

The Second Temple Is Dedicated

A joyous celebration was held to dedicate the Second Temple. A few older people remembered the First Temple from the days of their childhood and they felt sad. The Second Temple was not decorated as beautifully as the First. It did not contain the holy ark with its impressive stone tablets which once reminded Jews of their brit with God. The Holy of Holies was a dark, empty chamber reserved for God.

To almost everyone else, the new Temple was a great achievement. They had their Temple at long last, and

they sang for joy! They felt that God was again in their midst.

Difficult Times for the Returnees

The happy feeling, however, did not last long. A new enemy arose: the Edomites. They were a tribe who had settled on the land many years earlier. Now, they took over much of the land in the southern part of Eretz Yisrael. They raided Jewish towns, villages, and farmlands, and forced Jews out of their homes.

Another difficult problem was that there was no strong leader to guide and protect the Jews. The Persian king had appointed the governor of Samaria to take command of Judea. But he was not able to protect the Jews because he could not spare enough soldiers to patrol the territory to the south.

The high priest was the head of the Jewish community. But he was not a warrior, and he could do little to protect his people. He could do no more than appeal to the governor. In addition to the problem of safety, conditions on the farms were bad. Rains did not fall when they were most needed, and locusts gobbled up much of the produce. Poverty increased, while the payment of taxes continued.

These hardships were more than many Jews could stand. They were discouraged, and they failed to worship God sincerely. They did not turn to other gods, because they knew there was only one God. But . . .

1. Many failed to give one-tenth of their crops (which was called the *tithe*) to the levites. To earn their bread, the levites were forced to leave the Temple, and work elsewhere. As a result, the appearance of the Temple deteriorated.
2. Some Jews brought improper sacrifices, and priests offered them on the altar even though they knew it was wrong.
3. Some Jews became very careless in their religious practices, and even neglected to rest on Shabbat.
4. Some Jews married non-Jews, and their children grew up without the knowledge of God's teachings.

The Last Prophet

The brit with God was being slowly forgotten. The prophet Malachi, the last of the prophets, tried to teach the people that they must rebuild the land and must remain a holy nation.

He denounced the priests for their disrespect of God's holy altar. He scolded the Jews for failing to support the levites, and for their failures to keep the mitzvot. He urged his people to remember and obey the laws taught by Moses.

The people listened to Malachi with their ears, but their behavior remained unchanged.

Will the Dream Survive?

Things were not going well in Eretz Yisrael. Fortunately, Jews in other lands were concerned about their fellow Jews who lived there. The Babylonian Jews had prospered and lived in all parts of the huge Persian empire which, in those days, extended from India, all the way to the Mediterranean Sea, and into Egypt. Several Jews in Babylonia won high positions in the Persian government (which still ruled Babylonia at that time), and this was the cause of a good deal of jealousy.

A Jewish writer who lived much later composed the Book of Esther. In it he tells a story of Haman, the Prime Minister of Persia. Haman tried to convince the king — King Ahasueros—that the Jews were disobeying the laws of the land. This was not true, but King Ahasueros believed him and authorized Haman to destroy all the Jews in Persia.

Wicked Haman cast lots (*purim*) to decide on which day he would carry out his evil scheme. The lot fell on the 13th day of the Jewish month of Adar.

A Jew named Mordecai learned of the plot, and he reported it to his cousin, the brave and lovely Queen Esther. She was Jewish, but King Ahaseuros did not know it. Without first asking for permission, she went to the king and told him that she was one of the Jews whom Haman was planning to murder. The king forgave her for entering his throne-room without permission, and ordered that the Jews be saved and that Haman be hanged.

In thanksgiving to God, the Jews celebrate the joyous feast of Purim, on the 14th day of Adar. The 13th day of the month — the day which Haman had set for the slaughter of the Jews—is observed as a day of fasting.

The Book of Esther, in which this whole story is written, is read every year in the synagogue on Purim. In

Hebrew, it is called *Megillat Esther*, meaning the *scroll* of Esther.

The Jews of the Persian empire continued to live in peace. They were aware of the problems in Eretz Yisrael, and they urged Persian officials and the king himself to help the Jews.

Many Jews of Babylonia and other parts of the Persian empire even came to Eretz Yisrael to help personally. Two of these new arrivals worked a miracle. Of them, and their achievements, we will learn in our next unit.

SUMMARY OF UNIT III

Jews were happy to be God's people and rejoiced in their covenant with Him.

Most Jews, however, did not understand what the covenant — or, the brit, as we call it in Hebrew — really meant. They thought it meant that God had to protect them and bring them happiness. They believed that their part of the agreement was to do no more than celebrate festivals and offer sacrifices. But they were wrong.

The true prophets tried very hard to correct this wrong idea. They insisted that, to God, bringing sacrifices and celebrating holidays was not enough. More than religious ceremonies, God wanted the people to love Him and to serve Him by acting righteously, by worshiping Him alone, by being kind to one another and by helping everyone in need.

Most Jews paid little attention to the prophetic messages. Jews, like most other people, found it hard to change their habits. Besides, their non-Jewish neighbors seemed to get along well enough, and when they worshiped their gods, all they did was bring sacrifices. So, most Jews continued to worship God and idols at the same time. The people in power continued to take advantage of the weaker ones, and judges continued to accept bribes, and merchants continued to cheat. The real meaning of the brit did not make an impression on the Jews.

The Kingdom of Israel — the northern kingdom — was overthrown by Assyria 2,700 years ago, just as Amos and

Hosea had warned. These people became known as "The Lost Ten Tribes." We do not know what happened to all of them.

To the puzzled and frightened people of Judah, Isaiah offered an explanation of the tragedy. He said that God had punished the Kingdom of Israel because they were wicked. He did it by letting Assyria destroy them. Isaiah warned that the same thing would happen to the Judeans unless they lived up to the demands of the brit.

But, in Judah, as in Israel, men tried to keep the brit the easy way, with rites and sacrifices. They did not do it by living honest lives. Micah, Jeremiah, and Ezekiel repeated the warnings of Isaiah. Still, the people did not listen.

In 586 B.C.E., a little more than 2,550 years ago, the nation, the land, and the Temple were destroyed by the Babylonians.

The calamity made the people stop and think. Those who had been sent off to Babylonia found new strength to live on as Jews. From the prophet Ezekiel, they learned to respect the teachings of the prophets, to seek knowledge of God's mitzvot, and to meet for prayer and study. This became the foundation upon which the synagogue of the future was built.

Jews now began to understand the meaning of the brit, and made up their minds that they would live by its teachings. Encouraged by Ezekiel and by the Second Isaiah, they looked forward to return to their homeland — to Eretz Yisrael.

As Ezekiel and the Second Isaiah had prophesied, the Persians conquered the Babylonians and granted the Jews permission to return to Eretz Yisrael and to rebuild the Temple. While the majority remained in their comfortable Babylonian homes, thousands of Jews made an aliyah to Eretz Yisrael. Despite hardships, they built the Second Temple at the urging of the prophets Haggai and Zechariah. When Jews neglected the Temple and disregarded the mitzvot, Malachi reminded them of their duty to worship God and take care of the Temple.

The prophets loved not only God and Eretz Yisrael, but their fellow Jews as well. They knew that the Jews were no worse than anyone else. They called them wicked because only a few were able to meet God's requirements. They expected them to be much better than they were.

The same is true of the feelings of the prophets toward the Temple. They loved the Temple and its beautiful service. They objected only to the mistaken idea shared by many Jews that bringing sacrifices was enough to satisfy God! The prophets insisted that Jews must not only offer sacrifices, but must be righteous.

Malachi, who lived almost 2,500 years ago, was the last of the prophets in the Bible. We shall learn about new leaders, and their achievements in Eretz Yisrael, in our next unit.

2450-2300 YEARS AGO

EZRA AND NEHEMIAH BEGAN
PUBLIC STUDY OF TORAH, REBUILT
JERUSALEM'S WALLS, AND RE-
STORED REGULAR TEMPLE WORSHIP

THE HIGH PRIEST GOVERNED
ERETZ YISRAEL, SCRIBES WROTE
DOWN THE TANACH, AND MANY
JEWS MET FOR PRAYER AND STUDY

2300-2175 YEARS AGO - ERETZ
YISRAEL BECAME PART OF THE
GREEK EMPIRE. HELLENIC (GREEK)
CULTURE WAS ENCOURAGED.

Introduction

TORAH: THE FOUNDATION OF
THE JEWISH WAY OF LIFE

After the death of Malachi, almost 2,450 years ago, no other prophet appeared in Jewish life. In his place, another type of religious leader came to the fore, and took the place of the prophet. This new leader was a teacher.

The new leaders realized that *preaching*, as the prophets had done, would not change the lives of most Jews. They believed that in order to become true worshipers of God and to be faithful to the brit, all Jews would have to *learn* the teachings of God.

How were the Jews to learn the teachings of God? What *were* the teachings of God? Since the words were

2150 YEARS AGO - YISRAEL'S HELL-ENIZED SYRIAN RULERS FORBADE JUDAISM. THE MACCABEES LED THE JEWS IN A SUCCESSFUL REVOLT.

2100 YEARS AGO - YISRAEL WAS FREE AGAIN. PHARISEES TAUGHT JUDAISM AND ORAL LAW IN THE SYNAGOGUES. SADDUCCEES ACCEPT-ED ONLY WRITTEN TANACH LAWS, BUT BUILT A STRONG COUNTRY.

2050 YEARS AGO - YISRAEL BECAME PART OF THE ROMAN EMPIRE.

30 C.E. - THE ROMANS CRUCIFIED JESUS. HIS FOLLOWERS WERE CALL-ED CHRISTIANS, BUT STILL WORSHIPPED IN SYNAGOGUES.

70 C.E.- THE JEWS REVOLTED AGAINST ROME. THE TEMPLE WAS DESTROYED AND MANY CAPTIVES TAKEN AWAY. JEWS AND CHRISTIANS SEPARATED.

135 C.E. BAR KOCHBA LED ANOTHER TRAGIC REVOLT AGAINST ROME. ROMANS LATER BANNED JUDAISM BUT IT SURVIVED IN SECRET.

not yet written down, the people had no opportunity to read any of the holy books, not even the words of the prophets!

How did the new leaders over-come this problem? Unit IV will deal with this question.

200 C.E.-JUDAH HA-NASI COLLECTED THE MISHNAH (ORAL LAWS). JUDAISM HELD FIRM AS JEWS BUILT CENTERS OUTSIDE YISRAEL.

145

Modern scribes writing Torahs on parchment.
They are using quills for pens, as has been done
for over 2,000 years.

CHAPTER 16

A JEWISH WAY OF LIFE TAKES ROOT

Today, there are Jews in every part of the world. The largest and richest group lives in the United States.

Although most Jews today live outside of the State of Israel, almost all are very much interested in what is happening in Israel.

Twenty five hundred years ago, a similar situation existed. The largest and most important Jewish community was in Babylonia. And the Jews of Babylonia were very much concerned with what was going on in Eretz Yisrael.

Ezra Comes to Eretz Yisrael

When the Persian king, Cyrus, who had conquered Babylonia, gave the Jews of Babylonia permission to return to Eretz Yisrael, many thousands returned. But large numbers did not wish to go back, and so we find the number of Jews residing in Eretz Yisrael at that time very small. One hundred years after Cyrus permitted the Jews to return, not even 100,000 lived in the Holy Land.

Their dreams of building up a Jewish nation in Eretz Yisrael had faded. Even the very existence of the Jewish community was in danger.

But then, two Persian Jews arrived, and they began to lift the spirit of the community.

One man was famous for his wisdom, and for his knowledge of Jewish law. His name was Ezra. He was called Ezra the Scribe because his profession was to make copies of the holy writings. The king appointed him to strengthen the faith of the Jews by teaching them the religious laws and traditions.

Upon his arrival in Eretz Yisrael, Ezra felt sad at what he saw. Jerusalem's walls were broken down, the Temple was neglected, and Jews were married to non-Jews. The young generation knew nothing of God and His mitzvot. Even the Hebrew language was unknown to many. Jews had begun to speak the language of their neighbors — Aramaic.

Ezra realized that the people were disturbed by too many problems to be able to learn the laws and practices of Judaism at this time. So, he decided to wait for a better time. While waiting, he gathered a group of men to study the holy scrolls and prepare new copies.

To make the books easier to read, the new manuscripts were written in the kind of Hebrew letters we now use, instead of the ancient Hebrew script that had been used up to that time. Like ours, the new script had square-shaped letters. Archeologists in Eretz Yisrael have recently discovered coins inscribed with the ancient Hebrew letters.

Nehemiah Brings New Life to People

One day, Ezra received a summons to appear before a man named Nehemiah. When he arrived, he found a large group of men whom he recognized as the wealthy and respected leaders of the Jewish community.

Nehemiah stepped forward and produced documents proving that he was the newly appointed governor of Eretz Yisrael. Nehemiah then told the gathering that while serving as a high official of the king, he had learned of the troubles of his fellow Jews in Eretz Yisrael. To improve conditions, he had persuaded the king to appoint him governor.

Nehemiah announced that the first step was to make Jerusalem secure for its inhabitants. This must be done by rebuilding the broken walls around the city. He had examined the walls, and he knew just what had to be done.

All he wanted from the leaders who were assembled was help in finding the workers to do the job.

Some of the leaders were not anxious to help, but when the word of Nehemiah's plan reached the people, they were happy to volunteer their service.

The Work on the Walls

The old enemies of the Jews: the Samaritans, the Edomites, and other foreigners, tried to prevent the rebuilding of the walls. They interrupted the work by poking fun at the builders. At times, they even attacked them.

Nehemiah decided how to handle the situation. He armed his work crews. When an attack occurred, an alarm summoned the men to the place of danger. Dropping their tools, the workers took up their weapons and quickly drove off the attackers. The walls were finished in less than two months. Nehemiah was praised for being an able governor.

Nehemiah then promptly started a second project. He had noticed that many of the poor had sold themselves and their families as servants to the rich. They had formerly been city workers, farmers, or shepherds, but high taxes and bad crops drove them into debt. To repay what they owed, they had no choice but to give up their possessions and their freedom.

Helping the Poor and Enslaved

The governor again knew what had to be done. He assembled the wealthy Jews and reminded them that Jewish law did not permit a Jew to be enslaved to another Jew for more than six years. He also reminded them that the 50th year was the Jubilee year, according to the Bible. All property taken away had to be returned. It could not be held for more than 49 years.

The rich were not happy to hear all this. But Nehemiah was the governor, and they knew he enjoyed the full support of the king. They dared not refuse. The people were jubilant. Nehemiah was a great governor!

Temple Worship Revived

Now, Nehemiah undertook his third project. The Temple was being used, but needed improvement. The levites had grown few in number, and priests had grown careless in the performance of their duties.

Nehemiah reminded the people that it was their duty to give 10% of their produce to the Temple treasury. This was called the *tithe*. Governor Nehemiah appointed reliable officials to collect this tax. The levites returned to the Temple, and the Temple service was once again conducted with beauty and holiness.

Jerusalem Grows in Population

Nehemiah was far from finished. The city of Jerusalem, though protected by walls, had very few residents brave enough to settle in it. Should enemies attack Jerusalem, they feared the walls could be broken down. Men were needed to guard and protect the city. Therefore, Nehemiah *persuaded* some Jews to move to Jerusalem, and others were *forced* to do likewise.

The growth of Jerusalem attracted tradesmen to visit it every day of the week, including the Shabbat. Nehemiah knew that conducting business on Shabbat was forbidden by Jewish law. To keep the tradesmen away, he ordered the city gates locked from sundown on Friday to sundown on Saturday.

Nehemiah was now ready for his greatest task. He was ready to give Ezra his full support so that Jewish law would become the law of the land.

Torah Becomes the Jewish Way of Life

Before Rosh Hashanah, a great platform was erected in

the Temple court. The people watched the sacrificial service performed by the priests and levites, and then received a great thrill. Ezra ascended the platform, opened a scroll, and began to read aloud in Hebrew. Those who could not hear clearly, or could not understand the Hebrew, were told what was being read. The work of the scribes, who had labored with Ezra on arranging, correcting, and copying the holy scrolls, was now very useful.

For the first time, the Jews heard the Torah read publicly. For the first time, they knew that the Torah was their guide in life. They now knew what was expected of them as a holy people.

Some wept in quiet joy over their discovery. Others cried in bitterness over their past neglect of God's mitzvot.

Ezra noted the sadness of the people and comforted them. Gently, he reminded them:

> There is joy in celebrating our festivals. Soon the feast of Sukkot will be upon us. Prepare yourselves for the feast, set up your sukkot and prepare the symbols — the *lulav* and *etrog*.

After the people had returned to their homes, the leaders assembled again and pledged themselves to make Torah their official law.

As a first step, they agreed that Jews should divorce all non-Jewish mates. Carrying out this decision was so painful that some Jews left the country. But the agreement was enforced. Jews realized that non-Jewish idol-worshipers in their midst could only hurt them. It weakened their own faith.

A family in Israel celebrates the
holiday of Sukkot in their own sukkah.
Notice the old crates that were used for
walls.

The Book of Ruth

One of the books of the Tanach, the Book of Ruth, emphasized the fact that Jews did remain friendly to non-Jews. This book tells of a Moabite woman, named Ruth, who, though non-Jewish by birth, had married a Jew—a pious man—with the approval of the Jewish community. She won this right by demonstrating her love of God and her devotion to Jews. The Tanach shows the high regard it had for Ruth by declaring that one of her descendants was none other than King David!

The Book of Ruth speaks of the summer harvest in Eretz Yisrael which occurs around Shavuot-time, and for this reason it is read publicly on Shavuot.

Ezra and Nehemiah, both from Persia, worked together to make Judaism, as taught in our Torah, the accepted way of life. It proved to be one of the greatest accomplishments in our 4,000-year history. Torah became the basis of Jewish life. Since the days of Ezra and Nehemiah, over 2,400 years ago, Torah has remained the treasured guide of our people.

For a long time, peace and quiet prevailed in Eretz Yisrael. Suddenly, a new challenge appeared — a challenge to our Torah and to our Jewish way of life. Of that we shall learn in our next chapter.

CHAPTER 17

HOW THE TORAH WAS TESTED

The Making of the Bible

For about 100 years after Ezra and Nehemiah, the Jews lived in peace. The Persian governors allowed the high priest, assisted by a council of Jewish leaders, priests and scribes, to rule over the land. Agents of the high priest collected the taxes needed to pay the tribute due to Persia, and to support the Temple and the officials of the government.

In this peaceful period, the study of Torah flourished. Scribes busily prepared copies which they sold to all who could read, and could afford, the valuable manuscripts. Like Ezra the Scribe before them, these scribes gathered up the writings of the true prophets, and these, too, became part of our sacred literature. They also assembled other holy writings such as the Book of Psalms, the Scroll of Esther, the Scroll of Ruth, and similar writings. This last group of books was called the Holy Writings, and they became the third part of the Tanach.

And so, we now have the three parts of the Tanach: the Torah, the Prophets, and the Holy Writings. During the century that followed the lives of Ezra and

Nehemiah, the Tanach became the most valuable possession of the Jewish people.

How the Tanach Was Taught

With copies of the Tanach in their hands, the scribes traveled around to talk with the people of Eretz Yisrael. They encouraged, and even assisted, the residents of every town and village to establish meeting places. They were urged to meet, as their fathers and grandfathers had done in Babylonia. On the Sabbath and on festivals they would come together to listen to the words of the Tanach. The scribe, or some other learned person, would read the words and explain them. Jews would also come together on market days — usually Mondays and Thursdays—and then, too, parts of the Tanach were read.

More than any other part of the Tanach, it was the words of the Torah that were read at these get-togethers. In time, Jews learned to love the teachings of the Torah and to practice them. Many foreigners learned to admire the Jews and their way of life — so much so, that they adopted the Jewish religion!

While this was happening, Jews from the Persian empire continued to come to Eretz Yisrael, and the population grew larger and larger. Before long, Jerusalem became a large and prosperous city.

Little by little, the Jewish population of Eretz Yisrael spread to the south and to the west. Almost unnoticed, new towns and cities sprang up. Once again a Jewish nation was taking form and its citizens were living according to the mitzvot of God as taught in the Tanach. The prophets, the scribes, the scholars, and the teachers of Judaism had done their jobs well.

Alexander the Great in Eretz Yisrael

Twenty-three hundred years ago, a young Greek king, named Alexander, took his small army to battle against the powerful forces of Persia. And he defeated them! Alexander then conquered one country after another, and within a few years, all the peoples and nations once ruled by Persia became part of the new Greek empire.

For a time, the change did not affect Eretz Yisrael. The high priest merely sent the tax money to the Greeks instead of the Persians.

In fact, there are legends that describe Alexander's special friendliness to the Jews. According to one legend, one day, a messenger announced that King Alexander had arrived in Jerusalem. The high priest, dressed in his robes of office, and accompanied by the leading priests, came out of the Temple to greet the great conqueror. To the astonishment of all present, the king dismounted from his horse, and bowed before the high priest. Everyone was surprised!

The king's attendants were especially puzzled. They had expected the high priest to bow before their great and mighty king. Alexander then offered this explanation:

> This noble Jew (the high priest) once came to me in a dream and advised me how to win an important battle. I followed his instructions and won. I knew then, and feel sure now, that he is truly a man of God.

The reasons why the Jews admired Alexander, and were happy during his reign, were the following:

1. There was peace in Eretz Yisrael.
2. The Jews were allowed to continue their government under the leadership of their high priest.
3. They were permitted to continue the worship of God and the study of Torah undisturbed.
4. The tax that they had to pay to the Greeks was not any greater than what had been paid to the Persians. Besides, more traders were visiting Eretz Yisrael, and this added to the prosperity of the land.

The Greek Way of Life

What the Jews did not notice at that time was that small Greek colonies were being started throughout the Greek empire, including the lands around Eretz Yisrael. The colonists who moved into these territories were Greek soldiers and tradesmen. They were very proud of being Greek. They considered their language the most beautiful, their cities the finest, their literature the best, their art the highest, and their way of life better than all others.

Most Jews felt differently. Their Tanach, they were certain, was the greatest collection of books, and their way of life was the most pleasing to God. They, therefore, continued life very much as before.

Some Jews, wealthy landowners and big merchants, did business with the Greek tradesmen and with officials of the Greek government. They found it helpful to know the language and customs of the Greeks.

Occasionally, they took trips to other countries where they were able to see the beautiful Greek works of art. They envied the fine clothes, the comfortable homes, and the attractive theaters they saw. At times, they would even attend the exciting and popular Olympic games.

These games were held in a great, open stadium. Thousands of people would gather to watch the athletic contests. The ceremonies always began with sacrifices to the Greek gods, whose chief was Zeus. This was followed by the recitation of Greek literature. Then the contests began.

The exciting competition consisted of foot races, chariot races, wrestling matches, spear-throwing contests, and many others. The winners were awarded victory wreaths; and their names were proclaimed throughout the Greek world. The victors became great national heroes.

Jews who watched the games were deeply impressed. They may have felt uncomfortable during the religious ceremonies honoring Greek gods. However, they did enjoy the spectacle, and some Jews even envied the Greeks.

The Rise of Jewish Hellenists

Slowly, more and more of the Jewish upper classes

began to imitate the Greek style of dress. They got into the habit of reading Greek books, and attending Greek theater performances and athletic contests. Before long, they began to *feel* Greek. They thought of themselves as being different from other Greeks only in religion.

The Greek word for Greeks is *Hellenes*, and Jews who adopted the Greek-style of living became known as *Hellenists* — meaning, people who imitated the Greeks.

When King Alexander died, there were only a few Hellenists in Eretz Yisrael. But they soon grew in number.

Alexander's death led to a war between Alexander's generals who wanted to succeed him as king. One of these generals became king over Egypt and the nearby lands. (The year was about 323 B.C.E.) Another general took over the territory of Syria and became its king. He ruled over much of western Asia.

Both generals wanted Eretz Yisrael as part of their territory, and they fought over it. After several years of bloody fighting, Eretz Yisrael was won by Egypt.

While the war over Eretz Yisrael was taking place between the Egyptian-Greeks and the Syrian-Greeks, the armies of both groups came into contact with the Jews of the land. The Hellenists, in particular, mixed with them and adopted more and more of the Greek language and customs. Upper-class Jews, including prominent priests, imitated the Greek fashions. The number of Hellenists in Eretz Yisrael continued to grow.

Chasidim Rise in Opposition

The war between the two Greek armies on the soil of Eretz Yisrael brought great suffering to the Jewish population. While Jews were not involved in the actual fighting, their fields and homes were ruined, and their cattle was stolen or driven off. Many were injured and killed. Some were suspected by one side of helping the enemy, and were carried off as captives.

The horrible war led most Jews to hate the Greeks and their ways. They were convinced that their own way of life was much better. They realized that:

1. The Jewish religion, with its emphasis on one God, on righteousness, on justice, and on mercy, was far superior to the idol worship of the Greeks.

2. The beauty of form in art, which Greeks admired so much, was meaningless if it did not help people live as righteous people rather than as pleasure-seeking people.

3. Devotion to study of Torah and practice of God's mitzvot was much more important than engaging in games to prove one's physical prowess.

Gradually, Jews who were warmly attached to the Jewish way of life became known as *Chasidim*, which is a Hebrew word meaning "pious ones." The Hellenists, Jewish admirers of the Greek style, looked down upon the Chasidim. They were "peasants" in their eyes.

The Chasidim, on the other hand, regarded the Hellenists as unfaithful to God and traitors to their people.

The division between Hellenists and Chasidim grew sharp. The people were divided.

The grip of Torah on the lives of the Jewish people was being tested. How would the contest between Hellenists and Chasidim be decided?

CHAPTER 18

THE RIGHT TO BELIEVE IN AND PRACTICE JUDAISM

Chanukah

One of our best known and most loved festivals is *Chanukah* (Feast of Dedication). It is celebrated on the 25th day of the Hebrew month of Kislev. We light candles, chant blessings, sing joyous songs, play games, and distribute gifts. These ceremonies continue for eight fun-filled nights. Why all the fuss?

We know part of the answer: Judah Maccabee won a great military victory! True! But this is not the real reason, because we Jews do *not* celebrate military victories. Joshua's conquest of Canaan is not celebrated, and King David's successful wars against the enemies that surrounded Eretz Yisrael are not celebrated.

Judah Maccabee's victory is *not* celebrated as a military victory. The name of the holiday is Chanukah, and *Chanukah* means "dedication." What happened in Judea—in Eretz Yisrael—2,300 years ago, after the Greeks replaced the Persians as conquerors, will help us understand what kind of victory is celebrated on Chanukah.

The Jews of Egypt

For many years, the life of the Jews in Eretz Yisrael was very much the same. The high priest remained the principal leader. Usually, he was succeeded in office by his eldest son. The Jewish population grew in numbers, and most Jews followed the teachings of the Torah. Nevertheless some Jews were attracted to Hellenism.

One Jewish community in which Hellenism took root was Egypt. After the conquest of Egypt by the Greek king, Alexander, many Jews were taken there as captives. Some came of their own free will, because they thought they could make a comfortable living there.

In time, Egyptian Jewry grew larger and more prosperous. In the city of Alexandria, they built a magnificent synagogue. They observed the Jewish festivals, and they sent generous gifts to the Temple in Jerusalem. Whenever possible, they came to visit it.

Despite all this, the Jews of Egypt behaved like the Hellenists who lived in Eretz Yisrael. They dressed in Greek style, spoke Greek, read Greek literature, attended the theaters, and were spectators at athletic events. Gradually, the Egyptian Jews forgot Hebrew and could not even read the Tanach. They became completely Hellenized.

The Bible Is Translated Into Greek

A group of Jewish scholars then decided to translate the Hebrew Tanach into Greek! This event was so important that before long a legend grew up to explain how it was done.

The Egyptian king, we are told, learned from his chief librarian that Jews possessed a great collection of books that deserved an honored place in his library.

Thereupon, the king asked the high priest in Jerusalem to send him scholars to translate this collection—which happened to be the Tanach—into Greek. Seventy-two men arrived from Jerusalem. Each was placed in a separate room and was asked to write his own translation. When all had completed their assignments, the translations were found to be exactly alike. It was fantastic! They called it a miracle.

How the translation was *really* made, we do not know. But we do know that a Greek translation *was* made, and that Egyptian Jews accepted it and studied it.

Not only did Jews study this Greek translation of the Bible—which is called the *Septuagint*—but many Greek-speaking people did as well. After reading the Jewish Bible, a large number of non-Jews became believers in God. However, the number of Egyptian Jews who did accept the Greek style of living kept growing, and a few hundred years after the translation of the Tanach, Egyptian Jewry disappeared as a real community.

The Mad Dream of King Antiochus

Almost 150 years after the Greeks overthrew the Persian Empire (in about 333 B.C.E.), the Greek king of Syria defeated the Greek king of Egypt and took Judea—or Eretz Yisrael as we have been calling it—from his control.

King Antiochus Epiphanes of Syria—whose nickname was Epimanes meaning "the mad man"—became ruler of Judea. He dreamed of imitating King Alexander who had succeeded in conquering all the other nations.

But one mighty nation stood in the way of Antiochus.

That was Rome. Rome had shown its power by conquering all the lands of Europe and Africa bordering on the Mediterranean Sea, except Egypt.

Antiochus built up a huge army and equipped it with the best weapons. To get the vast sums needed, Antiochus not only taxed all the people in his kingdom, but also robbed the treasures of the various temples.

The Hellenistic High Priests

Some Hellenistic Jews took advantage of Antiochus's need for money. They bribed him to appoint a high priest whom they wanted in that high office. The loyal Jews were upset by this. In the 350 years since the Second Temple was erected, no ruler, be he Persian, Greek, Egyptian, or Syrian, had ever interfered in the choice of the high priest. But they could do little in the face of the armed Syrian soldiers who were now on the soil of Eretz Yisrael. A man named Jason was appointed to be high priest.

The Hellenistic high priest promptly permitted the Hellenists to build a gymnasium. There, statues of Greek heroes and gods were set up. There, young men, including priests, practiced for the Greek games, which included worship of Greek gods.

Before long, another group of Hellenists wanted to be in power. They gave Antiochus an enormous bribe, in return for which he appointed a new high priest whom they selected. His name was Menelaus. He was worse than Jason. Menelaus, the new high priest, had no respect for the Jewish religion, even though he was the official head of Judaism. He robbed the Temple treasury to pay what he had promised to Antiochus. He allowed statues of the king to be set up on the Temple grounds.

He did everything possible to turn all Jews into Hellenists.

Banning the Jewish Religion

King Antiochus was pleased with the new high priest. If he succeeded, Jews would become like all other Syrians!

But the Jews did not want to become like other Syrians. Instead, they stubbornly continued to worship God and obey His mitzvot.

Antiochus grew impatient. He was annoyed by the Jews who did not want to become Hellenized, and decided to put an end to the Jewish religion.

Antiochus decreed that to study the Torah, to rest on the Sabbath and to follow any Jewish religious practice was a crime! The punishment was to be *death!*

Jews Defy Antiochus

Many Jews ignored Antiochus' harsh decree. Some were caught and put to death. Others hid in the wilderness, in caves, or wherever they could find a safe hiding place. Syrian soldiers combed the land for them, and when they found a group, they waited for Saturday before attacking them. The Syrians had discovered that the Jews did not work on Shabbat. They would not even raise a weapon to defend themselves. The "brave" Syrian soldiers, therefore, decided not to take unnecessary risks by attacking Jews on weekdays!

Antiochus plundered the Temple treasury, carried off many holy vessels, damaged the golden menorah, and put out its eternal flame. He set up an image of Zeus (made to look like himself), on the altar of the Temple, and he sacrificed pigs upon it. Antiochus then ordered

his soldiers to go to every city, town and village, to set
up altars to Zeus, and to
force all Jews to eat the pig
meat that was sacrificed on them. This was more
than most Jews were willing to stand. To eat pig
meant that they had to violate the dietary laws.
These laws were part of the Torah and were very sacred.

The Maccabean Revolt

More and more Jews went into hiding, but the people
of the town of Modin (sometimes spelled Modiin) were
not afraid. They waited for the Syrians.

The Syrian soldiers came as expected, set up an altar to
Zeus, and brought a pig for the sacrifice.

The officer in charge then ordered Mattathiah
(sometimes called Mattathias), a priest who was the most
respected Jew of Modin, to obey the king's command by
sacrificing the pig to Zeus. Mattathiah stoutly refused.
When another man stepped forward to offer the sacrifice,
Mattathiah slew him. Then, Mattathiah's five sons, aided

by the townspeople, attacked the Syrian troops and slew all who did not flee.

Mattathiah then issued the call for rebellion:

Whoever is for God, follow me!

Mattathiah's sons and the men of Modin responded at once. Knowing that a large armed Syrian force would soon return, Mattathiah and his band headed for the hills and caves. Word of Mattathiah's bold act spread quickly. Syrian soldiers hunted for him, but could not find him. However, Jews from all over the land who came to join Mattathiah were guided by Mattathiah's scouts and found him easily enough.

Remembering that Syrians deliberately waited for Shabbat to make attacks upon the Jews, Mattathiah made a change in Jewish practice. Later rabbis approved of this change. If Jews are attacked on Shabbat, Mattathiah proclaimed, they must defend themselves. It is important that they do so if they, and the Torah, are to survive! Killing Jews was now no longer easy for the Syrian-Greeks.

Mattathiah soon died and was replaced by his son Judah, known as the "Maccabee." In Hebrew, *Maccabee* means "*hammerer.*" It also stands for the first letters of the Hebrew expression meaning: "Who is like You, O Lord, among the mighty?"

Both meanings describe Judah correctly. Like a hammerer, he crushed the Syrian troops. And his battle cry was a reminder to his small army that with God as their Protector, their small numbers could overpower the many thousands of Syrian soldiers.

Judah Maccabee and his followers were greatly encouraged by a little book that appeared at that time. It was the Book of Daniel which later became part of the Bible. This book describes Jewish heroes who were saved by God. Three pious Jews were thrown into a fiery furnace and, by a miracle, were able to walk out untouched by the flames. It also tells about Daniel who was cast into a lion's den and came out unharmed. The message of the book was that God performs miracles for those who believe in Him. He will destroy Syria!

Judah was a clever and a brave fighter. He knew the hills, valleys, hiding places, and narrow roads of Judea. Time after time, Judah's men ambushed the Syrians, destroyed the troops, and carried off their weapons. Judah's forces soon grew large enough to challenge and defeat large Syrian armies.

The First Celebration of Chanukah

In the year 165 B.C.E., Judah captured Jerusalem. He routed the Syrians and cleaned the Temple and its grounds. The vessels that had been lost, destroyed, or damaged were found and restored.

On the 25th day of the Hebrew month Kislev, a great ceremony was held to rededicate the Temple to the worship of God. The light of the great menorah, once extinguished by Antiochus, was rekindled. Songs were sung and sacrifices were offered to God. For eight days the festivities went on. When they were over, Judah proclaimed that this new festival, which became known as Chanukah, be observed at the same time, each year, for eight days.

It is not a surprise that beautiful legends began to circulate about Chanukah—the festival of the rededication of the Temple. The highlight of the ceremony was the rekindling of the golden menorah. No one could find the

A young boy carrying a torch from Modin to Jerusalem in celebration of Chanukah. This relay is repeated every year.

supply of special, pure, olive oil that was used for this purpose. Finally, only one small jar, enough for keeping the menorah burning for one day, was found. Miraculously, that little bit of oil lasted for eight days!

Another tale explaining the reason for celebrating Chanukah for eight days tells us that after the sons of Mattathiah, the high priest, defeated the Syrian-Greeks, eight iron spears were found in the Temple. The Maccabeans converted these instruments of war into instruments of peace. They stood them upright, inserted wicks in their tips, filled them with oil, and burned them in place of the regular menorah.

The eight-day Chanukah celebration was a sign to the Jews that they were now free to worship God according to the teachings of the Torah. They had gone to war, faced death, even killed to win that right. It was the first war men ever fought for the right to worship God!

How wisely did our forefathers use their freedom to worship God? Our next chapter will provide a partial answer.

CHAPTER 19

HOW HISTORY CHANGES OUR WAYS

On Shabbat eve, mothers in Jewish families place candles into carefully polished candlesticks, and light them. They then recite a prayer praising God for making us holy by commanding us to kindle the Sabbath lights.

Where, when and how did this beautiful tradition arise? It is not a biblical commandment! It came from a political party called the Pharisees, formed sometime after the celebration of the first Chanukah in 165 B.C.E. This political party is long dead, but its teachings continue to live in the hearts of faithful Jews.

The Struggle for Complete Independence

The Pharisees came into being because of a decision made by Judah Maccabee. While most of his followers were happy to be able to worship God in peace, Judah wanted to win complete independence from Syria.

So the war continued. New battles took place, and in one of them Judah was defeated and killed. His brothers continued the fight. All but one met their deaths in battles that were fought over a period of 20 years.

Finally, the Syrians gave up the fight. The fifth and only remaining brother of Judah Maccabee was then joyously acclaimed by the Jews as the ruler and high priest of the new and independent Jewish nation. His name was Simon. His descendants, who continued to lead the Jewish people, used the title "king," but Simon did not.

The family of Simon, now ruling the country, was called the Hasmoneans. They were so called because they traced their ancestry to a Jew named Hasmonai, and not to the beloved and popular King David. This caused some unhappiness among the Jews of Eretz Yisrael.

But the Hasmoneans were proud of their people and their religion. They strengthened the army, marched into the land of the Edomites, defeated them, and forced them to become Jews. They added territory to Eretz Yisrael by conquering Samaria, as well as several cities on the coast of the Mediterranean Sea. The wars and the victories pleased some Jews, but displeased others.

The Sanhedrin

To help govern the nation and make laws, the king called upon a national council consisting of 70 or 71 members. The exact number is not certain. This group was called the Sanhedrin.

In addition to advising the king and helping him carry out the decisions made, the Sanhedrin also served as the supreme court of Eretz Yisrael. The king, who was also high priest, chose the members of the Sanhedrin, and he presided over their meetings.

As expected, the Hasmoneans usually selected for membership in the Sanhedrin those who agreed with their own ideas. Most of these were wealthy landowners, high government officials, army officers, and wealthy businessmen. Among them were the leading priests who proudly traced their ancestry to Zadok, the first high priest in the Temple built by Solomon. These supporters of the king's policies became known as the Sadducees.

The Pharisees

The majority of the people opposed the Sadducees. Their leaders became known as *Perushim*, which probably means "separatists." They are called Pharisees in English.

The Pharisees, like the Sadducees, were happy to live in a land ruled by their own people, but they objected to the wars that were going on. They also were opposed to forcing non-Jews to become Jewish. To let the Hasmonean ruler and the Sanhedrin know how they felt about things, the Pharisees formed a political party.

The main interest of the Pharisees was not to make their nation great or glorious, but simply to help their fellow Jews become God's holy people. Therefore, they kept a watchful eye on the king and the Temple. When they saw anything improper being done, they made sure to let all concerned know about it.

The most important accomplishment of the Pharisees was their strengthening of the synagogue. The Sadducees were proud of the Temple, and the Pharisees shared their feelings. The Temple, however, was not enough to make the Jews into a holy people. For many, the Temple was too far away. At best, they could visit it only a few times during the year. Pharisees, therefore, encouraged the building of synagogues throughout Eretz Yisrael, and in the other lands where Jews lived as well. To these synagogues it was possible to come daily to worship God, learn the Torah, and perform the mitzvot.

A leader of the synagogue did not have to be a priest or

a wealthy person. Any learned man, even a humble laborer or farmer could be a leader of the synagogue. The synagogue taught the people to be more democratic. It taught them to respect any person who had knowledge of the Torah, and not only those who were rich or powerful.

Pharisees Encourage Study

The Torah and the other books of the Tanach were constantly studied in the synagogue. Adults often assembled for lessons taught in the evening by a learned Pharisee. However, this was not enough to satisfy the Pharisees. They demanded that *young* people come too!

Over 2,000 years ago, a law was passed *requiring* young city people to attend a school. It was the first law ever passed in any land compelling school attendance.

The Pharisees did not limit themselves to teaching the words of the Tanach. Much time was spent teaching the meaning *behind* the words. They explained and they interpreted the laws of the Torah and other books of the Bible in order to discover the *spirit* of the words, and the *purpose* of the laws.

The writings that were part of the Tanach became known as the Written Law, because many copies were available in written form and they could not be changed.

The teachings of the Pharisees were not all written down. Some were taught from mouth to mouth, from teacher to student. These teachings, that explained the Written Law, became known as the Oral Law. The Pharisees considered the words of the Oral Law to be as holy and important as the Written Law given by God to Moses.

One of the requirements of the Oral Law is the kind-

ling of the Shabbat light. The Pharisees had a special reason for introducing this practice. The Tanach prohibited fire on Shabbat, which meant that people had to eat cold food, endure the cold during the winter, and stay in the dark every Friday night.

The Pharisees, knowing that Shabbat was intended to be a day of delight, decided to change the life of the people by a simple reinterpretation. They said: the law which prohibits fire on Shabbat means that no fire may be *kindled* on the Sabbath. However, a fire started on Friday *may burn* through the night and continue on through the Sabbath day.

The new oral law made it possible to enjoy the Shabbat more fully. It fulfilled the spirit of the Sabbath law.

Most Jews accepted the teachings of the Pharisees, although no one forced them to do so. Yet, the influence of the Sadducees was so great, the Pharisees rarely succeeded in gaining a majority in the Sanhedrin. They found it difficult to make their teachings the law of the land.

Sadducees Increase Prosperity of Eretz Yisrael

The Sadducees found fault with the Pharisees. They said the Pharisees were not patriotic. The Sadducees also said that the Pharisees did not support the king's wars, and did little to promote prosperity.

The Sadducees were satisfied with the Written Law. They saw no reason for accepting the Oral Law taught by the Pharisees. They believed that all the interpretations were unnecessary and unimportant. To the Sadducees, the most important thing was to have a prosperous Jewish nation.

Supported by a majority of the Sanhedrin whose members were Sadducees, the Hasmonean leaders who had succeeded Judah the Maccabee and Simon believed that it was important for the nation

1. to extend its boundaries in all directions. In fact, they made Eretz Yisrael as large as it was in the days of King David.
2. to mint new coins (Some have recently been discovered by archeologists.)
3. to promote trade. This enriched the wealthy (mostly Sadducees) more than the city workers, farmers, and keepers of cattle (mostly followers of the Pharisees).
4. to encourage Hebrew as the national language. Educated people knew and used Hebrew both for writing and speaking. The average person continued using Aramaic as his everyday language.

The Hasmonean rulers were pleased by the support given to them by the Sadducees, and they paid little attention to the Pharisees and their teachings. Neither did they show much interest for the feelings and desires of the Jews over whom they ruled. As a result, the Hasmoneans, who were once loved and honored by their people, became tyrants in the eyes of the Jews. When two Hasmonean brothers started a war for the crown, the Pharisees and their large following became disgusted with the Hasmoneans.

Loss of Independence

The war between the Hasmonean brothers occurred at a time when unity was essential. It happened just as Rome was becoming a great power.

Rome had completed its conquest over Syria. The only land on the northern and western coasts of the Mediterranean still not controlled by Rome was Eretz Yisrael. It was certain that the Romans would soon seek to take possession of this territory. Even a completely united Jewish nation would have found it difficult to keep the Romans out. As a divided nation, it did not stand a chance!

After many hard-fought battles, a Roman general named Pompey marched his troops into Jerusalem, slaughtered those who opposed him, and captured the city. He then entered the Holy of Holies, the chamber of

the Temple reserved for God only. No man, other than the high priest, was ever permitted to enter it, and even he did so only once each year—on Yom Kippur. The Jews were deeply offended.

As in the days of the Syrian tyrant, Antiochus, a hundred years earlier, the Jews were helpless in the face of armed might. The independence of Eretz Yisrael was ended for the next two thousand years. It was restored in 1948.

Following the easy Roman conquest of Eretz Yisrael, Jewish life became increasingly hard. The Temple was maintained as before, but the high priest was under the thumb of the Romans. The ruler was either a Jewish king appointed by the Romans, or a Roman governor. Neither one concerned himself with the welfare of the people. Jews found life unbearable, and eventually they revolted. Part of that dramatic story we shall learn in our next chapter.

CHAPTER 20

THOSE WHO DESTROY AND
THOSE WHO BUILD

Is War Ever Right?

The problem that has troubled our world from days of old to this very day is war. Ever since the establishment of the United Nations, in 1945, the nations of the world have been seeking ways to stop nations from making war with each other. Thus far, the U.N. has had very little success.

Our prophets, Isaiah and Micah proposed a "simple" solution. They said that the way to stop making war is to stop making the instruments of war. They said we must turn *swords* — all weapons — into *plows*. By plows they meant all types of instruments to be used for peaceful purposes.

Not only Jews, but probably most people all over the world would agree with our prophets. However, no nation has, as yet, disbanded its army, not even the Jewish nation, Israel.

Let us go back in history and find out how our ancestors felt about peace and war when they were ruled by the Romans.

Jews Under the Roman Heel

You may recall, the Romans treated the Jews very badly. They killed those who opposed them, as well as many Temple priests who never took up arms. Pompey, the Roman general, even went so far as to enter the Holy of Holies! To make sure the Romans would remain masters of Eretz Yisrael, he appointed a Hasmonean named Hyrcanus as high priest and ruler.

Hyrcanus was a weak leader, and most Jews were displeased. They preferred his more vigorous brother.

But the Romans did not care about the feelings of the people they conquered. What the Roman rulers wanted most was power, fame, wealth and luxury.

You might think that it was good of the Romans to appoint a Hasmonean as high priest. Not so. The Romans knew that the Jews had rebelled against the Syrian-Greek king, Antiochus, a century earlier, and that they had won independence. Under the leadership of the Hasmoneans, they fought and won many wars. To keep the Jews from rebelling against them, the Romans allowed Hyrcanus, the Hasmonean, to retain his office. They knew this would satisfy some Jews who were strongly attached to the Hasmoneans.

At the same time, the Romans felt certain that Hyrcanus was not strong enough to ever lead a revolt.

To strengthen their hold on Eretz Yisrael, the Romans took away from the Sanhedrin the power to bring political prisoners to trial. Such trouble-makers were brought before a Roman court, not a Jewish one.

Herod, Son of Antipater

The Romans influenced Hyrcanus to keep as his chief

adviser a strongly pro-Roman Jew who was clever, rich, and ambitious. His name was Antipater. Antipater was a descendant of the Idumean people. His family was forced to accept Judaism when John Hyrcanus, son of Simon, was king.

Antipater appointed his son Herod as a local ruler. Herod was as cunning, ambitious and ruthless as his father had been. When the Romans wanted an extra-high tax, Herod collected it and kept a good part of it for himself. When some Jews tried to start trouble for the Romans, Herod had them executed without a trial. When asked to appear before the Sanhedrin to explain his illegal act, Herod came with a bodyguard. He defied the court, and was helped by Hyrcanus to escape untouched.

Many Jews were terribly unhappy and wanted to get rid of Rome and to win back their independence. During the first 25 years of Rome's rule over Eretz Yisrael, tens of thousands of Jews took up arms in support of Hasmoneans who tried to take back the throne. Each time, however, the Romans, often with the help of Jews like Herod, crushed the revolt.

In the last of this series of revolts, a youthful Hasmonean leader named Antigonus won the support of the nation. He defeated and captured Hyrcanus, sent him into exile, and declared himself king of Eretz Yisrael.

For a while, he was successful, but the Romans had other plans. They appointed Herod, their most reliable ally and friend, to be king—even though he had no right to that office. With the support of Roman troops and hired soldiers, mostly foreigners, Herod defeated Antigonus and became king of Eretz Yisrael.

Herod the Builder

Herod's success pleased the Romans. The way he ruled Eretz Yisrael pleased them even more. Throughout his long reign, which lasted for more than thirty years, Herod behaved like a true Roman despot. Herod sought power, fame and wealth, and he taxed the people heavily. Most Jews remained poor, but Herod built fine palaces for himself, such as the one on top of Masada which is a popular site for people visiting Israel today.

He even built new cities. One of these was Caesarea, named in honor of the Roman emperor. In the course of time, it was abandoned and fell into ruins. Recently, the Israelis rebuilt parts of Caesarea. Located on the Mediterranean, it has been turned into a showplace which many tourists visit.

To add to his fame as a builder, and, at the same time, to please the Romans, Herod erected theaters and hippodromes in many cities, including Jerusalem. He knew, of course, that most Jews objected to such amusement places, especially in Jerusalem. Herod, however, was not at all concerned with the feelings of the Jews.

Herod is Suspicious

Herod, like other Roman rulers, governed the land with an iron fist. Anyone even suspected of wanting to revolt was imprisoned. Most of the surviving Hasmoneans were murdered. He even put one of his many wives to death. She was a beautiful Hasmonean princess named Mariamne. He loved her, but he suspected her of disloyalty, and she was put to death at his command.

Three of Herod's own sons met the same fate! He was so suspicious of everyone that before long the land was

An aerial view of the fortress of
Masada, built by King Herod.

filled with his spies. Herod himself often went out in disguise so he might discover how the people felt toward him. Anyone suspected of opposing him was quickly imprisoned or executed.

The officials that Herod appointed were all meek people. Their first duty was to serve him—the king—and not the people.

One act that displeased the people was the removal of the high priest. Herod appointed one who would be loyal to him. As a result, many Jews lost their high regard for the Temple, and their anger at Herod grew. Herod also took away all real power from the Sanhedrin. They had nothing to say about serious matters involving life and death.

Herod Bows Only to Rome

Knowing well that he held his high office only because the Romans wanted him there, King Herod did everything possible to please them. The cities he built or rebuilt were generally renamed in honor of prominent Romans, and they were settled by gentiles. These non-Jews were given the jobs of constructing and maintaining the cities.

To please the Romans even more, Herod put up many statues of Romans. He knew that Jews did not like this, because images were forbidden by the second of the Ten Commandments. But, he didn't care about Jewish feelings.

Herod also pleased the Romans by sending them money, gifts and even troops. Naturally, Herod was a great king in the eyes of the Romans. They called him Herod the Great, and increased the territory over which he ruled. To the Jews, however, he was Herod the Wicked!

Herod's New Temple

The one gift that Herod gave to Jews was a new Temple. In place of the 500-year-old Temple building, he erected a truly magnificent structure, and surrounded it with beautiful courts. The new Temple thrilled every visitor. It brought a spirit of joy and pride to the Jews.

But, cruelly or stupidly, Herod spoiled his glorious achievement by mounting a golden eagle over its main gate! The eagle was the symbol of Rome, and it reminded Jews of their enslavement to Rome.

Mounting the eagle was also an act of desecration. It was an unwanted object on a holy Jewish site. The eagle was an image, and the Ten Commandments did not allow images to be erected.

Some desperate Jews tried to tear down the hated image. Herod, who by then was close to death, ordered the men burnt alive! Herod died a few years before the year 1 C.E., hated and despised by his people.

The Essenes

The Jews had been treated very badly by Herod and were very bitter. Some gave up all hope of ever again enjoying life. A group of men, known as Essenes, withdrew from society and went off to form communities of their own. They devoted their entire lives to the fulfillment of the mitzvot. They spent their working days in tilling the soil. The rest of the time they spent in study, prayer, and in keeping themselves ritually clean. They bathed daily in cold water and dressed in white. They watched their food very carefully to make sure it was *kosher*. They followed strict rules of burying the dead. In every way, the rules of the Torah governed the lives of the Essenes.

The Essenes yearned for peace and justice, and established communities based on these principles. However, they could not accomplish these goals for the rest of Eretz Yisrael. They consoled themselves by saying that this was the responsibility of the Messiah—God's anointed—to whose speedy arrival they looked forward.

Herod and the Pharisees

The majority of the Jewish population belonged to the Pharisee group. A small number believed that it was necessary to fight against Herod and the Romans who supported him if they were to gain complete freedom. Like the Essenes, they hoped for a Messiah to come and save them, but they were not willing to depend upon that alone. They prepared themselves for revolt.

But most Pharisees accepted the conditions laid upon them by Herod and the Romans. They did not complain as long as Herod allowed them to worship God and obey the laws of the Torah.

They were permitted to observe the Sabbath and holidays. Whenever possible they paid a visit to the Temple in Jerusalem, especially on the three major festivals: Pesach, Sukkot and Shavuot.

Children learned how to live a good Jewish life from their home life. They saw mother prepare the daily food according to strict Jewish law, and, as they sat down to the family meals, they joined father in thanking God for the food they were about to eat.

Friday was an unusually busy day for mother and

daughters. The house was thoroughly cleaned. Food for the Shabbat, which included fish, fowl, or meat was prepared. The table was elaborately set. The Shabbat lamp was scrubbed, filled with oil, and kindled before dark.

Shabbat was a quiet and peaceful day. Fathers and sons went to the synagogue where they listened to selections from the Torah and Prophets being read and explained. When they returned home, they stopped to glance at the *mezuzah* on the doorpost—just as they had done when they left. The parchment in the mezuzah was inscribed with the words of the Shema. It was a constant reminder of God and His commandment to study Torah.

Walking through the streets of the city, the quiet and peace of the Shabbat was felt all over. If they lived in Jerusalem, as almost a million Jews did, they were sure to look in the direction of the Temple and be filled with pride as they saw the beautiful sight.

On holidays, they visited the Temple in family groups. When they arrived, the family separated. Mother and sisters entered the court for women, while father and sons went to the court reserved for men. The custom of separating men and women in many synagogues today grew out of this Temple practice.

Hillel Wins Hearts of the People

When the boys were old enough, they attended school and studied Torah. Adults often attended an academy taught by learned Pharisees.

While Herod was still alive, many people loved to attend the lectures of one of the wisest and kindliest Jewish sages of all time — Hillel. To this day, Hillel's name is pronounced with love, and his legal opinions are highly respected and accepted.

In his own day, Hillel was the great leader of his people. He was loved by all people. Even Herod, who suspected anyone to whom the Jews looked for leadership, never bothered Hillel. Herod, like everyone else, knew that Hillel was a man of peace. Without seeking it, Hillel rose to fame and honor, and he won the hearts of his people.

Hillel's Early Years

Hillel was born and educated in Babylonia where a large Jewish community still lived peacefully. Jews also lived in Europe, in Egypt, and in the northwestern part of Asia, called Asia Minor. The Jews in Asia Minor spoke Greek and studied the Bible in Greek. The Babylonian Jews did not speak Greek, and they did not study the Bible in Greek. Like their fellow Jews in Eretz Yisrael, the Jews of Babylonia spoke Aramaic and studied the Tanach in Hebrew.

A traveler passing through Babylonia told Hillel of the great Pharisaic teachers in Jerusalem. Hillel left his home and family, and like many other Babylonian Jews, made the aliyah to Jerusalem.

Hillel in Jerusalem

Hillel never regretted his decision. The beautiful sights he beheld on his arrival in Jerusalem thrilled him. But it was not long before he learned of the poverty under which so many of the people lived, and how King Herod oppressed them. These facts, however, did not trouble Hillel too much at that time. He was so pleased and happy to see Jews worshiping God.

Most of all, Hillel had come to Jerusalem in search of learning. He wanted to know more about the Written and the Oral Law. And he was happy, because his search was quickly rewarded.

In the academies of learning, Hillel found wise and kindly teachers. They fulfilled his highest expectations. After finishing his day of manual labor in order to earn his bread, he devoted every spare moment to the study of the Torah.

Hillel's Reputation Grows

Hillel's devotion to the Torah and his skill in applying its teachings to the everyday problems of the people soon became known in Jerusalem and elsewhere. He was chosen as head of an academy in Jerusalem, and shortly thereafter was chosen as the leader of the Sanhedrin. These important positions gave Hillel the opportunity to improve the spiritual life of his people. Despite Herod's severe laws, Hillel taught his followers to be happy.

As head of the academy, Hillel explained many biblical laws that had puzzled other teachers. He was kind and patient and always helped his students understand the lesson.

Hillel once said: "If I am not for myself, then who will be for me?" And everyone understood that their beloved teacher wanted each individual to consider himself important and to demand his rights.

However, it was not enough to obtain rights for oneself only. Other people were equally important. And so Hillel also taught: "But if I am for myself only, what am I?" Hillel meant that a selfish person was lower than a human being. Everyone must help everyone!

Hillel wanted everyone to be educated. He, therefore, said: "If not now, when?" He insisted that it was wrong to postpone one's studies.

Hillel treated everyone kindly. When he realized that priests were not sure how to conduct the Temple services properly, he clarified the rules. When the poor came for assistance, he graciously shared his food. When people came for guidance, he laid aside his work to help them. When people with bad manners tried to anger him, Hillel won them over with his patience.

When non-Jews wanted to become Jews, he explained in very simple language the most important teaching of Judaism. He said: "What is hateful to you, do not do to your neighbor." Then he continued: "This is the most important teaching of the Torah. Everything else is merely an explanation of this law."

As the head of Sanhedrin, Hillel saw to it that some rules of the Torah were reinterpreted so that people could live with less difficulty. He made it easier for merchants to borrow money; for people who sold their homes, he found a way by which they could change their minds and buy them back within a year at the same price.

As chief judge in the Sanhedrin, he interpreted the laws in such a way that it became difficult for innocent people to be convicted. He also made punishments lighter.

Hillel was the complete opposite of the ruling king. Herod destroyed his people. Hillel built up their spirits. He taught peace and lived in peace. He helped the troubled spirit of his people.

Herod is forgotten by most Jews, but Hillel lives on as a shining light.

CHAPTER 21

CHALLENGES TO BELIEF

The Power of Unity

In 1967, the Arab countries surrounding Israel waged war against the Jewish state and hoped to destroy her. Israeli men and women who were able to fight entered the army. Others, including the old and the very young, did everything in their power to keep all essential industries, as well as the farms and schools, in full operation.

Jews living in all parts of the world united behind their fellow Jews of Israel. They raised large sums of money to help the Israelis through the crisis, and they called upon their governments to help Israel.

The unity among Jews was rewarded. After six days of war, Israel emerged victorious. She defeated those who planned to destroy her, and was safer and stronger than ever before.

Our ancestors in Eretz Yisrael faced a similar situation 1,900 years ago. The difference was that *then*, the Jews were unable to unite despite the clear danger that threatened them.

Unity Is Destroyed

When Herod died, shortly before the year 1 of the common era (C.E.), the unity of the country was broken. Herod had six sons. His wish, as recorded in his will, was that Eretz Yisrael be *divided up* among three of his favorite sons.

One of his sons was to rule Judea and Samaria, which included Jerusalem and the Temple area. A second son was placed in charge of the territory of Galilee, the northern part of the country. A third son was to rule a small area called Panias (also called Banias), in the far north, where the Jordan River begins.

The unity of the Jewish people was badly hurt. When Herod's sons proved how weak they were as rulers, the unity of the people suffered even more. Now, Rome stepped in and replaced these sons of Herod with their own governors. Each governor made life very hard for the Jewish people. They suffered greatly.

Looking for the Messiah

Many Jews began to feel that things were so bad that surely God would now send His Messiah to deliver them. They hoped that he would be the long-awaited descendant of King David. But, they would have been quite content even if the Messiah were a general, like Judah Maccabee—a brave man who could defeat the Romans.

The Essenes did not feel the same way. They were concerned with purity, and religious practices. They were not worried about winning a military victory over the Romans. They looked forward to the Messiah whom they pictured as a great teacher of righteousness, or a noble high priest who would turn the hearts of the Jewish people to God.

In one of their towns, near the Dead Sea, some of the Essenes kept busy making copies of the books of the Tanach. They also wrote commentaries on some of the biblical books, and even wrote new books explaining their beliefs. For safekeeping, the Essenes wrapped their scrolls in cloth, placed them in huge jars, and stored them in caves.

In 1947, an Arab boy, searching for a lost goat in the hilly country about seven miles from Jericho, accidentally discovered some of these ancient scrolls written about 2,000 years ago.

The whole world was excited! Archeologists quickly organized search parties and found many more of the precious scrolls. Famous all over the world, these ancient scrolls are called the "Dead Sea Scrolls," because they were found near the Dead Sea. These scrolls can be seen in museums in Israel and in several countries.

By studying the Dead Sea Scrolls, scholars learned that the words in our Tanach are practically the same as they were in ancient times, even though the books had been copied by hand thousands of times! Copyists of the Tanach were extraordinarily careful!

Joshua: "The Messiah"

A young Jew named Joshua, who lived with his parents, Joseph and Mary, in the city of Nazareth in Galilee, was a great admirer of the Essenes. Like them, he loved God and Torah. Like them, he accepted the rule of the sons of Herod, and later, of the Roman governors.

Like members of the Essene sect, Joshua believed that the world would soon come to an end, that God would punish the sinners; and that He would establish a world of peace and justice. He believed that God would send

Workmen at the modern mineral plant at Sodom on the Dead Sea. The mountains in the background are in Jordan.

His Messiah to save the righteous people. The Messiah would be a peaceful teacher of righteousness.

Before long, Joshua (later called Jesus) was convinced that *he himself* was that Messiah. To save as many sinful Jews as possible, he travelled around the Galilee (to the north of Jerusalem) and urged his fellow Jews to love God and obey Him. Joshua was a great preacher and a kindly man. Soon, he won many followers.

To win more people to his way of thinking, Joshua and his disciples came to Jerusalem shortly before Pesach. The city was crowded not only with its own large population, but with thousands of pilgrims. These visitors had come from all parts of Eretz Yisrael and from many other lands to celebrate Pesach in the Temple. This was a mitzvah most Jews were anxious to observe: to visit the Temple three times each year — on Pesach, Sukkot and Shavuot.

Pontius Pilate: Roman Governor

The Roman governors who were appointed by the Roman emperor to rule over Eretz Yisrael were called *procurators*. One of the most cruel of all the procurators was Pontius Pilate. He was appointed by the Roman Emperor Tiberius, to govern the affairs of Judea. The city of Jerusalem was within the province of Judea. Pilate did not care one bit about the religious feelings of the Jews; and the Jews hated him.

When Joshua and his small group of followers came to visit Jerusalem, Pontius Pilate was there. Pilate knew the city would be crowded with Passover holiday visitors, and his soldiers were on guard, ready to stop any revolt that might get started. He kept careful watch over a group called the Zealots (meaning: passionate people). Pilate's spies warned him that they were plotting a revolt.

Pilate also kept his eye on Joshua. He had heard that Joshua considered himself the Messiah. He did not bother to learn what kind of Messiah Joshua believed himself to be, and what he planned to do. Pilate thought that this young Jew from Galilee, where Jews were most rebellious, might be planning to lead another revolt against Rome. He was worried about this, because Joshua's followers were calling him God's anointed one. To avoid trouble, Pilate accused Joshua of treason and ordered his execution. The common Roman method of putting people to death in those days was crucifixion. People were nailed to two pieces of wood shaped like a cross, and were left to die.

The Rise of Christianity

Most Jews who witnessed Joshua's painful death felt sorry for him, just as they did for the thousands of other innocent Jews who had been crucified by the cruel Romans.

The famous Jewish historian, Josephus, witnessed and recorded the events of those tragic years, but he never mentioned Joshua's name. And there is no known report of Joshua's death recorded by the Romans who crucified him.

Nevertheless, the crucifixion of Joshua turned out to be one of the most important events in world history. It was the starting point of Christianity, and became one of the main reasons why there is anti-Semitism in the world.

While the Jews and Romans attached no special importance to Joshua's life or his death on the Roman cross,

Modern Bethlehem where Jesus was born nearly 2,000 years ago.

his devoted followers reacted differently. Sorrowfully, they watched Joshua suffer and die. And they found it impossible to believe that their beloved teacher whom they regarded as *the* Messiah was really dead. They preferred to believe, instead, that he ascended to heaven, and that he would soon return to the earth to save the wicked world. They kept the memory of Joshua alive by holding meetings at which they repeated his teachings. They traveled around, telling everyone who would listen about the Messiah.

Joshua Becomes Jesus Christ

About 25 years after the death of Joshua, a Greek-speaking Jew named Saul was deeply impressed by Joshua. He was convinced that Joshua *was* the Messiah. He felt that all people—Jews and non-Jews alike—would be saved from going to hell (and would go to heaven) if they would only believe in Joshua and try to imitate him by leading good lives.

Since Saul spoke Greek, he called himself by his Greek name — Paul. He also changed the name Joshua to its Greek form—Jesus. Paul always spoke of Joshua the man as Jesus Christ. Christ is a Greek word meaning "the anointed one" or "the Messiah."

It became Paul's mission in life to tell people that they could be saved from punishment for their many sins. He traveled far and wide. He preached in many synagogues scattered throughout the vast Roman empire.

Paul appealed especially to non-Jews who had been taught by Jews to believe in one God. He taught these Gentiles that to believe in Jesus one did not have to become a Jew or observe the laws of the Torah. Not all

Jewish believers in Jesus agreed with Paul on this point. Many believed in Jesus *and* in the laws of the Torah at the same time.

Paul also changed the Jewish belief in one God. Jesus Christ, Paul insisted, was God's Son, and he was like God Himself. The believers in Jesus Christ who thought of Jesus as the Son of God, became known as Christians.

Jewish-Christians who lived in Palestine opposed Paul's teachings for many years. They considered themselves Jews who differed from their fellow Jews only in their belief that Jesus was the Messiah. But Paul was successful in winning many Gentiles to his Christian teachings, and taught his followers to believe in Jesus as a god.

The New Testament

Christians added new books to the Tanach — to the Jewish Bible. They called these new books, the New Testament, meaning the new covenant.

The name "New Testament" expressed the Christian belief that God broke His brit with the Jews and made a new covenant—a new testament—with the Christians. This happened, Christians were taught, because God became displeased with the Jews when they refused to accept the Christian belief that Jesus was the Christ (Messiah) and the Son of God Himself.

Most Jews throughout history could not, and did not, believe that Jesus was the Messiah or the Son of God. We have always believed that our brit with God is in force and that, some day in the future, a true Messiah will appear to help save the world.

The New Testament also wrongly blamed the Jews for the horrible death which Jesus suffered. It said that the

Roman governor, Pontius Pilate, was not responsible, and that the Jewish leaders were responsible for the crucifixion. Because of these teachings, Christians began to hate Jews. They called Jews "Christ-killers," and, throughout history, many Christians persecuted Jews because of it.

The fact is that while Pontius Pilate was the procurator, no court of the Jews, not even the Sanhedrin, had the power to order the execution of a political offender. The Romans had taken that power away from them. Therefore, what Christians had been taught for 2,000 years was not true. The Jews were not responsible for the death of Jesus!

The New Testament is the main source of the charge which claims that Jews are responsible for the death of Jesus. But these books were written many years after his death, and the writers could not have known the real facts.

To Revolt Or Not to Revolt

At the time of Jesus, and, in the years following his death, there were many small Jewish parties within the Jewish community. Quite often, the parties disagreed with each other. And, very often, the people in the same party did not agree with each other.

One very important issue on which the Pharisees, the Sadducees, and the smaller parties could not agree upon was whether the Jewish people should revolt against Rome.

The question arose because Jews had always wanted to be an independent nation. But, more important, at this time it was a problem because the Romans were treating them very badly, and life was becoming unbearable for many.

The Romans showed their cruelty in many ways. They
1. Crucified, or killed in other ways, not only Jesus, but thousands of others who were suspected of plotting a revolt.
2. Appointed men as high priests and to other offices in return for bribes. They also took bribes from others who wanted favors.
3. Levied heavy taxes on the people.
4. Robbed the Temple of vast sums of money.
5. Favored the Gentiles who lived among the Jews.
6. Introduced Roman symbols, which Jews regarded as images, into Jerusalem.

Despite the harsh, and often unjust, treatment which Jews suffered at the hands of the Romans, most Jews were not prepared to revolt.

One Jewish party—the Sadducees—even sided with the Romans! They were the wealthy people. They included many of the officers of the government and the leading priests who believed that the Romans would protect them and their property. Many fellow Jews regarded the Sadducees as oppressors of the poor, and hated them as much as they hated the Romans.

Another Jewish party, led by the Pharisaic teachers, believed that peace with Rome was best for the Jews. To strengthen the desire for peace, the Pharisees, under the leadership of Joshua ben Gamala, proclaimed that all young Jewish boys study Torah in school.

Some groups opposed starting a war with Rome because they believed that the Romans were too powerful. Others wanted to wait for a God-appointed Messiah to save them and their fellow Jews from the heavy yoke of Rome.

War with Rome

A large number of Jews, however, agreed with the Zealots. They were anxious to revolt, and they waited for the right opportunity. In the year 65, the Roman governor stole a large sum of money kept in the Temple. Not having the power to stop him, the Jews jeered at the governor. As punishment, the Roman soldiers attacked and killed many Jews.

Shortly thereafter, a leading priest raised the banner of revolt. His first action was to persuade his fellow priests to stop the practice of offering sacrifices in the Temple in honor of the Roman emperor. The Romans were angered by this move, and an army was sent into Jerusalem to deal with the problem. The Roman army was routed, and the victorious Jews seized large quantities of weapons from the Romans and prepared for war.

The Romans, and their emperor Nero, knew that the war would be hard to win. Therefore, they made careful plans for an all-out attack. An able and experienced general named Flavius Vespasian was appointed, and he assembled a large and well-equipped army. It took the Romans more than a year to complete their plans.

In the meantime, the Zealots in Eretz Yisrael tried to strengthen their own forces. But, instead of selecting a leader with military experience, they made the mistake of choosing Flavius Josephus to be in command of the defense of Galilee—the northern part of Eretz Yisrael. Josephus was a scholar more than a soldier, and he did little to train the men in his command or to build forts. He was more interested in himself than in his country.

When the Romans finally attacked, the Galilean Jews fought bravely. But it was not long before the well-trained forces of Rome overcame and butchered the Jewish defenders.

Josephus surrendered. He was taken prisoner and called upon Jews to follow his example—to give up their fight against Rome.

The Jews called Josephus a traitor, and they despised him. He is remembered today only because he wrote a history of the Jewish people in which he gave a careful description of the war against Rome in which he personally had participated.

Jerusalem Falls

With the Galilee conquered, the Roman general, Vespasian, proceeded slowly and cautiously toward Jerusalem. On the way, he learned that the Jews of Jerusalem were divided; that they were fighting each other. They were even destroying the stores of food they had saved up.

Vespasian slowed down the pace of his army in order to give the Jerusalemites more time to weaken themselves. He then sent his son Titus to strike the fatal blow at the quarreling Jews. Leading some of Rome's best legions, Titus arrived in Jerusalem and set up huge war machines to batter down the walls of the city. And little by little, the walls tumbled, and the city was destroyed.

The Arab village of Rama in Upper Galilee.

The Jews fought bravely. Often, they rushed out to drive off the attackers. The fighting was fierce, but the Jewish fighters were no match against the Romans with their superior equipment.

The climax was reached in the year 70 C.E. The city fell to the Romans. It was the very same day and month on which the Babylonians destroyed the First Temple in 586 B.C.E. On the ninth day of the Hebrew month of Av (Tisha B'Av), the Second Temple went up in flames. Jewish leaders were imprisoned or executed; thousands were led away captive to be sold into slavery. Tens of thousands more fled from Eretz Yisrael.

It took another three years for the Romans to crush the spirit of Jewish revolt completely. In these years a few hundred thousand Jews lost their lives. The last fortress to fall was a stronghold on top of a steep mountain called Masada, located near the Dead Sea. Today, the site, having been partly restored, is visited by a constant stream of Israelis and tourists from all countries.

Without a Temple, and without a government of their own, how did the Jewish people manage to survive this great calamity?

It seemed impossible, but it happened. It was like a miracle!

The worker of the miracle was Rabbi Yochanan ben Zakkai, a follower and admirer of Hillel. Of him, and his great achievements, we shall learn in our next chapter.

The calamity of the year 70 did not dry up the desire for Jewish independence. What happened? That too, we shall soon discover.

CHAPTER 22

JEWS BECOME A PEOPLE
OF THE WORLD

Crisis of the Year 70

One of the worst crises in the history of our people was what happened in the year 70. Hundreds of thousands of Jews were killed in battle. Additional tens of thousands died of hunger and disease. Large numbers of Jews were sold into slavery, and many more escaped to distant lands.

The Temple was left a heap of ashes by the Roman conqueror. The Sanhedrin was abolished. The land became the property of the Roman ruler.

Jews remaining in Eretz Yisrael, as well as Jews in other countries, were without leaders, without a government, and without a strong organization. How did our people survive this calamity?

Yochanan ben Zakkai

One of the men who fanned the spark of hope and kept Judaism alive was Rabbi Yochanan ben Zakkai. He was a follower of the great Hillel. Like Hillel, Yochanan ben Zakkai loved the Jewish way of life, he loved its laws and customs, and its hope for a world of peace for all people.

Living in Jerusalem during the war with Rome, Yochanan ben Zakkai had advised his people to make peace with the Romans. When the Zealots decided to continue the rebellion, he thought it best to leave Jerusalem and to go to Yavneh, a small town far from the fields of battle. (On some old maps Yavneh is called Jamnia or Jabne. It is located on today's maps between Tel Aviv and Ashdod.) There, along with a few other teachers, Rabbi Yochanan established an academy for the study of both the Written Law (Tanach) and the Oral Law.

When Jews learned that Jerusalem *and* the Temple had been destroyed on the ninth day of Av (Tisha B'Av), they went into deep mourning. Yochanan ben Zakkai, however, knew that the disaster would come, and he was prepared for it. He reminded the mourners that the prophets had taught our people to worship God even without a Temple. What God wanted most of His people, Yochanan said, was for Jews to be kind and just. This could be accomplished even without a Temple.

Synagogues Established

To make it possible for his fellow Jews to survive as God's chosen people, Rabbi Yochanan ben Zakkai urged that synagogues be established in every city, town and village. In these synagogues, there were to be schools to teach the laws and traditions of Judaism to children, young people, and adults. In the synagogues, law courts were to be established to settle disputes and to enforce the laws of Judaism. In the synagogues, the poor were to be given money and food to keep them alive and well. In the synagogues, people were to meet and discuss the welfare of the community. And, in the synagogues, Jews were to assemble for regular worship.

But synagogues were not enough to keep our people united. Teachers were needed to teach, judges were needed to judge and leaders were needed to guide the people. Rabbi Yochanan, therefore, ordained Jewish scholars to serve as rabbis and teachers. He also declared that he and 70 other scholars would serve as a *Sanhedrin* — a sort of Supreme Court — to interpret Jewish law.

Because there were no Jewish calendars, no one knew in advance when the holy days would occur. To enable Jews to observe the festivals and fast days at the proper time, the Sanhedrin announced the dates of all holidays from month to month.

Rabbi Yochanan ben Zakkai and the Sanhedrin that met in Yavneh had no power to carry out their decisions. But, the influence of these scholars was so great that Jews were willing to follow their instructions and their advice.

New Leaders in Yavneh

Rabbi Yochanan ben Zakkai was an old man when he came to Yavneh. In a few short years, he achieved remarkable success. Then, he retired in favor of Rabbi Gamaliel. Before his death, he blessed his pupils with these words: "May the fear of God guide your actions as much as the fear of man."

The new head of the academy and Sanhedrin in Yavneh was given the title *Nasi* (prince). Rabbi Gamaliel was not as learned a man as Rabbi Yochanan ben Zakkai. Nevertheless, he was respected by the members of the Sanhedrin and all Jews everywhere because of his fine character, and also because he was a descendant of Hillel.

Bet Shearim was the place where Judah the Prince lived. In this town, the Sanhedrin held its meetings during the second century. A few years ago, archeologists discovered a cemetery at Bet Shearim where many members of the Sanhedrin were buried. Above you can see one of the burial places that was cut into the mountainside.

Rabbi Gamaliel contributed to the strengthening of Jewish life by doing the following:

1. He interpreted Jewish law in the same way as Hillel and his followers. This made it easier for the people, because the law of Hillel was more lenient.
2. He required each community to appoint a council to collect the funds needed to support the synagogues, schools, courts, and all other services necessary for the welfare of the people.
3. He appointed qualified rabbis and judges.
4. He changed the order of the worship services to meet the new conditions of life. Prayers were added for the rebuilding of Jerusalem and the Temple.

Jupiter in Jerusalem

Guided by the Nasi and the Sanhedrin in Yavneh, Jews remained loyal to their religious beliefs. They kept hoping and praying that the day would come when they could rebuild their holy city, Jerusalem, and erect a Third Temple on Mount Zion.

Early in the second century, a rumor circulated that the Roman emperor was about to let their prayers come true. They waited, but it was only an empty rumor. There was nothing that the Jews of Eretz Yisrael could do to free themselves from the rule of the Romans.

Jews in Egypt, Cyprus, and elsewhere tried to join some of the revolutions against Rome. These attempts were not successful, and many lives were lost. The Jews in Eretz Yisrael did not participate in these revolutions against Rome. They did not want to antagonize the

Romans, and kept hoping that, as a result, they would be permitted to rebuild Jerusalem and the Temple.

In the year 130, hope for Roman permission to build a third Temple suddenly died completely. The Roman emperor announced that Jerusalem would be rebuilt, but as a *Roman* city. A temple *would* be erected, but it would be dedicated to the Roman god, Jupiter!

The Jews of Palestine were deeply hurt. Turning the holy city, Jerusalem, into a pagan shrine was an attack on God and on the Jewish religion!

Rabbi Akiba Becomes the Leader

Despite their love of peace, Jews prepared for war. They found a leader in the aged Rabbi Akiba, the most learned, the most loved, and the most respected Jew of his time. He was not a warrior; he was a scholar.

Akiba had spent his youth as an ignorant shepherd. Then, he married beautiful Rachel, the daughter of a wealthy Jerusalem landowner, and she urged him to start studying. For the next 25 years, he studied the Written and the Oral Law. In the course of these years, he became a great and wise teacher. Thousands of students flocked to his school in Bnai Berak, which is located near Tel Aviv on today's map.

Rabbi Akiba suggested many new ways of making the law suit the needs of his people. His interpretations were so numerous that many people wondered whether Akiba was teaching a new form of Judaism!

An old legend describes Moses coming back to life and sitting in on a lecture given by Rabbi Akiba. Moses listened to Akiba's explanations, but could not understand them. To Moses, it seemed that Akiba was teaching a new Torah instead of the Jewish Torah, which he,

The ruins of a synagogue at Capernahum on the shores of the Kinneret (Sea of Galilee). Many Jews prayed in this synagogue during the lifetime of Rabbi Gamaliel.

Moses, had written. Moses calmed down, however, when he realized that the Torah taught by Akiba was, indeed, the same, but the conditions of life had changed, and the law had to change along with it.

Akiba's aim in life was to teach the people to understand and to love the Written and Oral Law, and to worship God by observing the mitzvot faithfully. He devoted many years to collecting and arranging the new laws, that were part of the Oral Law, in a manner that would make it easier for people to learn and remember it.

Akiba was a great patriot, too! He was a great fighter for independence! Despite his advanced age, Rabbi Akiba called upon the Jewish people to revolt against Rome because it had desecrated the holy city of Jerusalem.

Simeon Bar Kochba Wages War

In the year 132, thousands of Akiba's students put aside their books, and took up the sword. They joined tens of thousands of other Jews in following a leader who reminded them of Judah Maccabee. This clever and brave fighter was Simeon bar Koziba (a son, or native, of the town Koziba). Rabbi Akiba admired him greatly. He even believed that Simeon was the Messiah, and he renamed him, Simeon bar Kochba (Son of the Star).

The Romans were not prepared for a revolt. Bar Kochba and his men fought bravely and well, and before long they recaptured Jerusalem and other cities. Hadrian, the Roman emperor at the time, sent in his best generals and a great many new, well-trained soldiers. Slowly but surely, the Romans retook the cities captured by Bar Kochba.

In the year 135, the Romans penetrated Bar Kochba's last stronghold and killed all the defenders, including Bar Kochba. None of the Jews who lived in the countries bordering on Palestine came to the aid of their fellow Jews.

We are still learning more and more of what happened during these years. Recently, archeologists unearthed some of Bar Kochba's letters, army orders that he issued, and coins minted during those war years.

Rome Outlaws the Jewish Religion

As in the year 70, when Jerusalem was captured and the Temple was destroyed, now, too, hundreds of thousands of Jews died in battle. Many others fled the country and found new homes in strange lands. And many thousands of others were taken captive and sold into slavery.

The Roman emperor was still not satisfied. To prevent further uprisings, Eretz Yisrael was made a part of Syria. While Jews continued to call their homeland Eretz Yisrael, from this time on, the name Palestine became the official name of the country and was so called on all maps and in all literature.

The Roman emperor decreed that the Jewish religion could no longer be practiced. Like the Syrian tyrant Antiochus, 300 years earlier, the Roman emperor, Hadrian, did not permit the observance of the Shabbat, the circumcision of boys, and the study of Torah. He also abolished the Sanhedrin that had been meeting in Yavneh, and he prohibited the ordination of rabbis. Anyone caught disobeying these laws was put to death.

He ordered that Jerusalem be rebuilt as a *Roman* city, and that a temple in honor of the Roman god, Jupiter, be erected on Mount Zion where the Temple originally built by Solomon once stood.

The spirit of the Jews remained firm. Some openly, and many secretly, defied the Roman laws. Rabbi Akiba was caught teaching Torah, and was tortured to death. With his last breath, he proclaimed that there was only one God. "Shema Yisrael," he cried aloud as he was about to die,"*Adonai Elohenu, Adonai echad.*"

Another rabbi was burned alive wrapped in a Torah scroll. A third, caught ordaining rabbis, was killed on the spot. The story of ten of these great martyrs is recorded in the Yom Kippur prayer-book, but the number of martyrs who refused to obey the laws of the Romans ran into the thousands. Fortunately, the cruel emperor Hadrian, died, and his successor was more lenient. Most of the harsh laws against the practice of Judaism were withdrawn.

Sefira and Lag Ba-Omer

Bar Kochba's war has remained an important event in Jewish history, and, as a result many legends have come down to us about this period in our history. Some of the stories concern the 49 days between Pesach and Shavuot. This period is known as *Sefira*, which is a Hebrew word meaning "counting."

The first of these 49 days is the second day of Pesach. On that day, a "measure" (in Hebrew called an *omer*) of newly, ripened barley was brought to the Temple as an offering. Each day thereafter was counted one by one, until 49 days had passed. Then came the holiday of Shavuot—on the 50th day.

This procedure of counting the days of the omer is called *sefirat ha-omer*. The 33rd day of the omer was called *Lag Ba-Omer*. The letters which form the Hebrew word *lag* add up to 33.

Two stories are often told to explain why Lag Ba-Omer is an important day. One tells of a terrible plague that struck the scholars in Bar Kochba's armies. Happily, it ended on Lag Ba-Omer.

Another tale tells of Rabbi Simeon ben Yochai who, like Rabbi Akiba, hated the Romans. He too, was a great teacher. On Lag Ba-Omer he found out that the Romans were about to arrest him. He fled to a secret cave, and remained there for many years, studying the Torah. His students visited him secretly on Lag Ba-Omer and spent the day in study. Rabbi Simeon ben Yochai, it is said, survived by eating the fruit of a carob tree that grew nearby.

Some Jews today celebrate Lag Ba-Omer by going on outings as did the students of Rabbi Simeon ben Yochai, and by eating carobs as did Simeon ben Yochai himself. In Israel, on Lag Ba-Omer, many Jews make a pilgrimage and hold a grand celebration near Simeon's burial place.

The Jewish People Lived On

The war of 135 weakened the Jews of Palestine. Their beloved city, Jerusalem, was turned into a pagan shrine. Many of their academies and synagogues were destroyed, and the cities in which they had lived were in ruins. The numbers of pagans and Christians in the country kept growing, while the Jewish population was getting smaller. Poverty was seen all over the land, and the spirit of the Jews was at low ebb.

Yet, wonder of wonders! The Jewish people lived on! Determined to live as God's chosen people, they worked at rebuilding their community. They reopened academies for the study of Torah, and synagogues for worship. They re-established the Sanhedrin under the leadership of a Nasi and strengthened the practice of Judaism. Before long, Jews who had been living in other lands, turned once again to the Nasi in Eretz Yisrael for advice and guidance.

Always Hoping for the Messiah

One thing did change, however. Jews stopped hoping that they would regain their independence or that they would be able to build a third Temple very soon. So, instead, they devoted their energy to keeping the Jewish people alive. One way of keeping up their hope was to look forward to the great day when the Messiah would finally arrive. On that day, our ancestors felt, the Jewish people from all parts of the world would return to Eretz Yisrael, and they would rebuild the country. When that day arrived, they believed all peoples of the world would learn to worship God, and to live in peace.

While waiting for the Messiah, our ancestors were not idle. They kept working to bring love and peace into the world. They worked hard trying to live by the law of God. Sometimes they succeeded; sometimes they failed. In the process, they left us a good heritage. In our next volume we will learn more about it.

SUMMARY OF UNIT IV

About 70 years after the first Temple was destroyed, the Jews built a second Temple. Besides offering sacrifices, Jews wanted to worship God by learning more about God.

Scribes, headed by Ezra, began the difficult task of collecting all the known writings, selecting those they regarded as holy (inspired by God), correcting, and editing them. Centuries later, the Tanach was officially accepted as the Jewish Bible.

In the course of many years, our people gradually learned to assemble on Shabbat, Yom Tov, and even on market days (Mondays and Thursdays). They met in public buildings, which became known as synagogues. There, they worshiped God and heard a portion of the Torah and the Prophets read and explained.

For 200 years, Ezra's followers continued their work. They wanted Jews to know about the brit and to live up to it.

The Persians ruled Eretz Yisrael after the Babylonians lost power. Under the Persians, the high priest and his council governed the land. Jewish religious beliefs and practices were not interfered with. Eretz Yisrael was at peace.

Then, the Greeks overthrew the Persian empire. Many Jews began to admire the Greeks. They accepted their way of life. These Jews, who were called Hellenists, turned from the study of the Tanach and the practice of mitzvot.

About 2,175 years ago, the Greek ruler who controlled Syria took away Eretz Yisrael from the Greek ruler in Egypt who until then had been in control. The Syrians tried hard to make Jews live like Greeks. After winning over some of the wealthy Temple priests, the Syrian king, Antiochus, decided to Hellenize all Jews. He appointed a high priest who would help him.

Most Jews would not change their way of life. Jews rose in revolt under the leadership of Judah Maccabee. After a bitter struggle, Eretz Yisrael became an independent nation, ruled by the Hasmoneans.

Several parties developed among Jews. The important ones were the Pharisees, the Sadducees and the Essenes. Most Jews followed the Pharisees. They developed the Oral Law, which explained the Written Law. The Sadducees believed only in the Written Law.

The Hasmoneans (descendants of the Maccabees) generally sided with the Sadducees, and, as a result, lost their popularity. In later years, they became tyrants. The Pharisees and their followers disliked them.

The Romans conquered the Greeks. They took advantage of the division among Jews, and seized control of Eretz Yisrael about 2,050 years ago.

Jews resented the Romans, and rioted against them often. The Romans crushed these uprisings.

Again Jews were divided. Some, known as Zealots, were determined to revolt against Rome. Most Jews followed the Pharisaic teachers who thought it unwise to revolt. They devoted their energies to building synagogues, and to worship and study. Pharisaic teachers continued to interpret the Written Law and to develop the Oral Law.

Like all Jews, the Pharisees suffered at the hands of the Romans. They planned no revolt, however. They felt confident that God would send His anointed king (Messiah) to deliver them.

The Essenes devoted their efforts to living pure lives and to performing the mitzvot. They did not care who ruled the land. They expected God to send His Messiah to bring peace and righteousness to the world.

Influenced by the Essenes, Jesus thought of himself as the Messiah. The Romans considered him a revolutionary, and they put him to death on the cross.

One of Jesus' followers, Saul, later named Paul, said Jesus was *the* Messiah and was the Son of God. Paul said that it was *not* necessary to observe the mitzvot. He taught people that they would be "saved" if they believed in Jesus as the son of God and the savior of mankind. Some Jews and many gentiles accepted his teachings. They became known as Christians.

In the year 66, the Zealots revolted against Rome. In the year 70, Jerusalem fell, the Second Temple was burned, and hundreds of thousands of Jews were killed. Many Jews fled from the land, and the land was impoverished. The surviving Jews rebuilt their homes, industries, farms, schools and synagogues. The study of Torah and the performance of mitzvot continued.

Index

227

Student's Notes

Student's Notes

Student's Notes

Student's Notes

Student's Notes

Student's Notes

Student's Notes

Student's Notes

Student's Notes

Student's Notes

Student's Notes

Student's Notes

Student's Notes

Student's Notes

Student's Notes

Student's Notes

Student's Notes